To Amy Kearns — woof! woof!

Solomon Kent

Solomon Says
Observations of an Innkeeper Dog

Joanne M. Anderson

CLAY CORNER PUBLISHING
401 Clay Street SW • Blacksburg, VA 24060

This book is dedicated to
the volunteer, dog guide puppy-raisers
who give so generously of their time and energy,

and to

the nation's innkeepers who work so hard
to provide travelers with friendly, safe
and comfortable places to rest.

✩✩✩✩✩

One dollar from the sale of each book sold
will be donated to:

Leader Dogs for the Blind
Rochester, Michigan

Solomon Says

Observations of an Innkeeper Dog

Joanne M. Anderson
Photography by Andres R. Alonso

Solomon Says
Observations of an Innkeeper Dog

By Joanne M. Anderson

Published by:
Clay Corner Publishing
401 Clay Street SW
Blacksburg, Virginia 24060
U.S.A.

All rights reserved. No part of this book may be reproduced or transmitted in any form or by any means, electronic or mechanical, including photocopying, recording or by any information storage and retrieval system, without written permission from the author, except for the inclusion of brief quotations in a review.

Copyright © 2001
By Joanne M. Anderson

First Edition
Printed in the United States of America
By RR Donnelley & Sons Company

Library of Congress Card Number: 2001116013

ISBN 0-9706542-0-0

Dogs
Innkeeping
Bed & Breakfast
Labrador Retrievers
Dog Guides

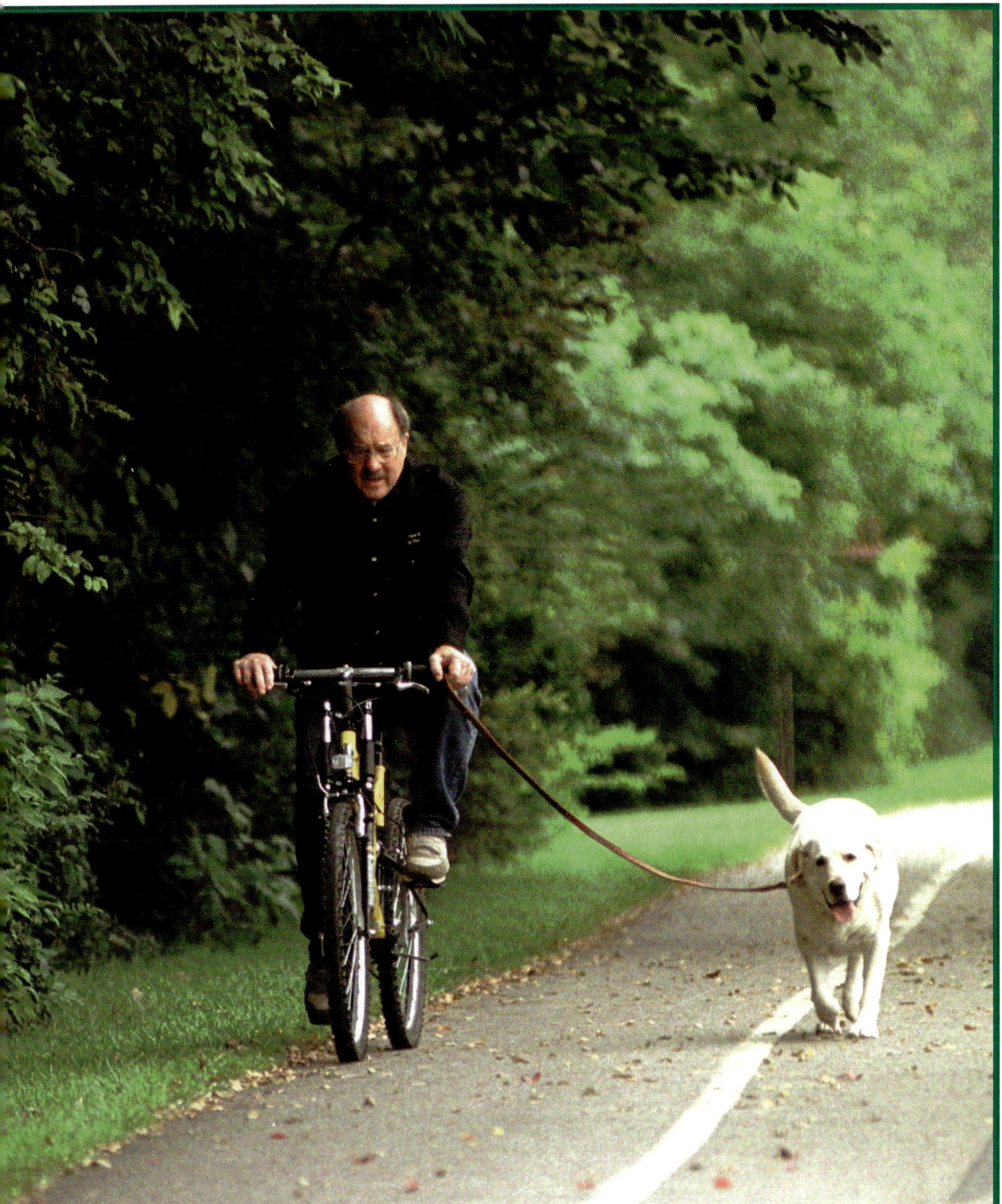

CONTENTS

Acknowledgements	10	Wake-Up Call	32
Introduction	12	The Kitchen	34
Growing Up Is Hard To Do	14	Serving Breakfast	36
Leader Dog School	16	Breakfast Cleanup	38
My First Week by Kent	18	Cooking and Baking	42
Business Overview	22	Recipes	46
Business Plan	24	The Guest Room	50
Mission Statement	26	The Bathroom	52
Innkeeper Quarters	30	Decorating	54
		Amenities	58
		Furniture	60
		Housekeeping	62
		Laundry	64
		Reservations	66
		Business Travelers	68
		Special Events	70
		Negotiation	72
		Checking In	74
		Checking Out	78
		Employees	80
		Money	82

Maintenance	86	Vacation	116
Repair and Renovation	90	The Future of Innkeeping	120
Safety	92		
Advertising	94		
Media Relations	98		
Names	100		
Writing	102		
Photography	104		
Tipping	106		
Health and Well-being	108		
Innsitting	114		

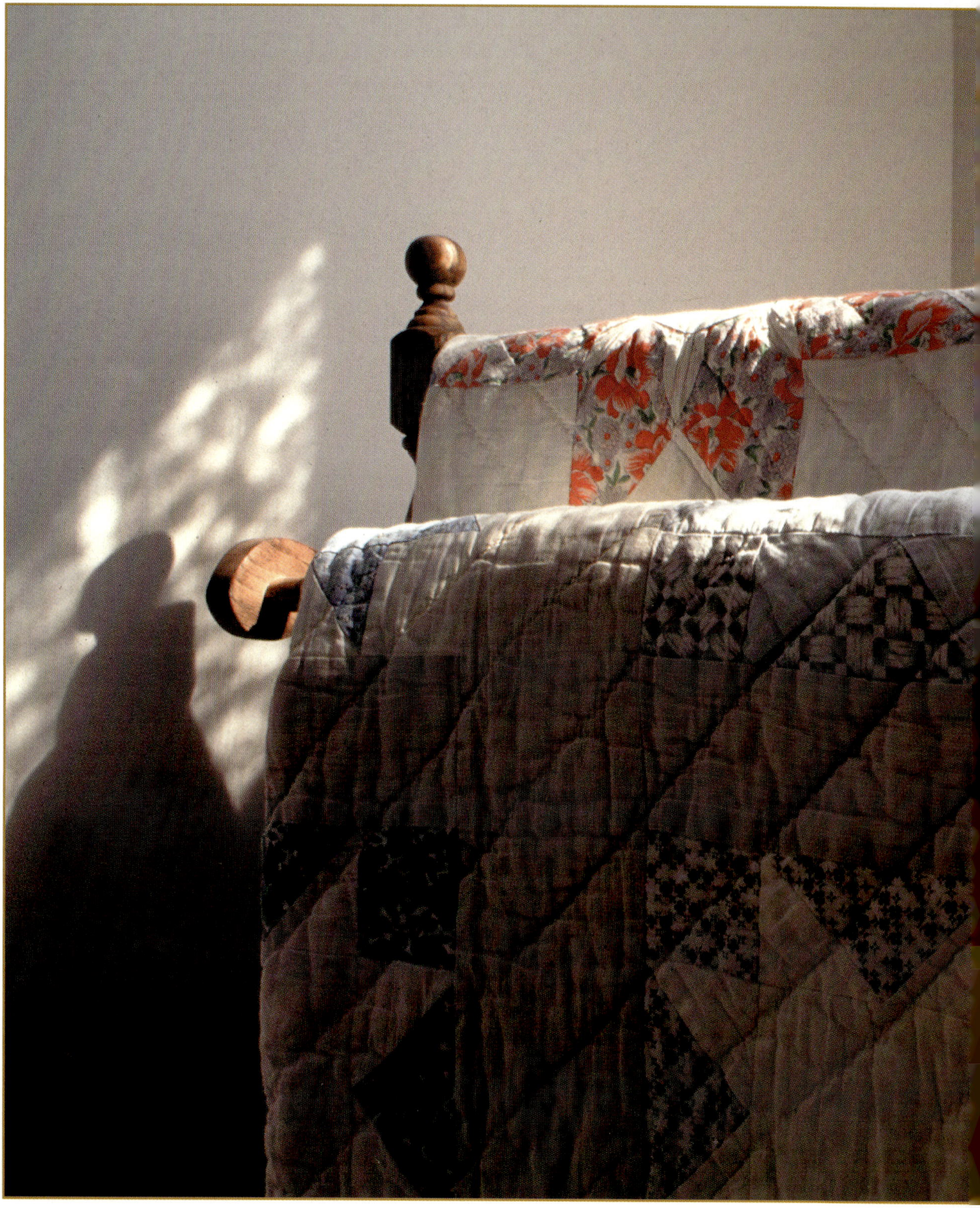

You are holding this book because my friend and free-lance colleague, Andres Alonso, encouraged me to finish it, and he handled the photography, layout and design. His advice and candor have been valuable all along the way.

The staff at Clay Corner Inn is to be commended for keeping things operating smoothly so I could write *Solomon Says Observations of an Innkeeper Dog*. Amy Crawford, Robyn Furey, Betty Lucas - thank you especially for your commitment to the bed and breakfast every day.

My sister Debbie Cate's honesty from the beginning contributed significantly to the final concept. My husband John's patience and support helped bring this to reality.

Ted and Bea Ake read the book at a preliminary stage and offered valuable comments and ideas. Thanks to Bruce Jensen and Sandy Bosworth for their interest and advice.

A big thank you goes to Leader Dogs for the Blind for providing Kent as an understudy dog for Solomon.

Joanne

Introduction

> I don't suppose it will knock any of you people off your perch to read a contribution from an animal. Mr. Kipling and a good many others have demonstrated the fact that animals can express themselves in remunerative English .... But you needn't look for any stuck-up literature in my piece. A yellow dog that's spent most of his life in a cheap New York flat ... mustn't be expected to perform any tricks with the art of speech.
>
> Preface to *Memoirs of a Yellow Dog*
> O. Henry, 1906

Ditto from a yellow dog that's spent most of his life in a nice bed and breakfast inn!

This book chronicles observations in my job as an Innkeeper Dog, which is my second of three careers - so far. I'm only seven. My third career is writing, this book being produced on the heels of a successful newsletter column. These two jobs are my choices and are well-suited to my personality. My first career path was not mine to decide, and I think it's best that I was able to change lines of work early in life.

My mother was owned by Leader Dogs for the Blind. My littermates and I were born in Virginia to be Leader Dogs - not a bad life for a dog when you consider that you have a constant human companion, you get to go places most dogs never see, you are admired for good looks and brains, and you are in a privileged position to serve.

The drawbacks of being a dog guide include not sitting on seats in a moving vehicle, not getting edible treats, and not chasing things, any things, not one tiny thing. While these activities may seem trivial in the great scheme of an admirable life of service, they have all become quite meaningful to me.

After many months of training to be a Leader Dog, a flight to the Michigan headquarters and eight days there, I was diagnosed with bilateral hip dysplasia and therefore not physically suitable to continue

Leader Dog training. The position of Innkeeper Dog was available and I readily accepted.

Actually, I had moved to this bed and breakfast just a few weeks before my Michigan trip. My people, John and Joanne Anderson, purchased the property in June 1994. They are referred to throughout the book as Mister Innkeeper and Lady Innkeeper, or simply Mister and Lady. They also have had multiple careers; she in technical writing and public relations; he in engineering and executive management.

The original property was composed of three houses, a garage and a heated swimming pool. Two adjacent houses were acquired in 1995, and the whole place was re-named Clay Corner Inn in July 1996. In May 2000, we bought a little house that borders two of the other houses.

So, we three basically started out together learning the business, defining our various roles and so on. I remember the first guests, four days after we moved in.

That first morning I stuck close to the kitchen to see how this food thing was going to work out for me, uh, excuse me, for the guests, for the guests, of course. (Some editor should have caught that little *faux pas*.) With boxes everywhere and guests seated at outdoor tables, Lady started reading a booklet.

"What are you reading?" asked a curious guest who popped her head in the kitchen door.

"The directions to the coffeemaker," responded Lady, adding that neither she nor Mister Innkeeper drank coffee so she had never made any. I'm not sure this was the smartest thing to say under the circumstances. I mean, these folks were chewing their nails outside for some coffee!

Our innkeeper careers were launched. For my part, I fell quite naturally into breakfast cleanup activities, socializing and yard and pool maintenance. It became evident over time that I needed an assistant. As luck would have it, 2-year-old Kent was just leaving Leader Dogs because of hip dysplasia. He came here as a junior innkeeper dog, and I'm training him.

Kent wrote one chapter for this book called My First Week. He also got in on a couple photo shoots. He's a quick learner and a very good assistant.

Solomon

1

Growing Up Is Hard To Do

Born and bred to be a Leader Dog for the Blind, I started my training at the tender age of 16 weeks. I had on a little collar to which was attached a six-foot, leather leash. I wore a blue bandanna with "Future Leader Dog" in red letters.

It was late October 1993, and we lived in the mountains outside Blacksburg, VA. Up the driveway we walked. I jumped on every leaf that moved and tried to make friends with every bug on the pavement. Sometimes we went into town to experience more activity, noise, traffic and people. Life was fascinating, and the world seemed like one big playground.

After a few weeks of these walks, however, I began to realize that jumping at leaves and investigating insects was not what I was supposed to be doing. Boring as it sounds, my mission was simply to walk without being distracted. Walk to the left and slightly ahead of Mister or Lady.

I did this to the best of my ability, and on a good day, I was able to go 10 or 12 feet without tangling the leash around their legs while running after something. A pine needle, tidbit of paper, my tail, anything that moved or looked interesting, which is basically everything on the ground.

Slowly but surely, I developed a little restraint. I learned to lead, to move forward confidently and assertively without reacting to all of nature's toys around me.

Photo by author

I also learned to sit, lie down and stay, sometimes. Most of this was easy because Mister and Lady got so incredibly excited when I did something right. "Lavish the praise" is their philosophy.

They got equally as excited when I took a pee outside. They put me in the same place on the side of the house several times a day – when I woke up, before I ate, after I romped around a lot, between naps, before I went to bed. Even now, every night, just before going to bed, they put me outside, I act appropriately, and they smile and tell me what a good dog I am.

I started jumping on people when I was about 6 months old. I don't understand Mister and Lady's great aversion to this since I wasn't jumping on them. They actually set people up to come to the front door just to teach me to stay off. I got more praise for keeping my paws on the floor, so I eventually quit jumping.

I went to obedience school, which appeared to me to be just another lost opportunity to play with lots of dogs. I tried to pay attention. I got a certificate for the class, but I wasn't the star pupil.

Photo by author

David Cate, 2

Because I was training to be a Leader Dog, I went almost every place with Mister and Lady – restaurants, hotels, discount and grocery stores, the Post Office and the bank. I attended church and concerts. I learned to be very patient and quiet.

I barked once in the Virginia Tech library when I saw someone's feet a few aisles away – thought they might want to play. I also barked at a bear in a natural history museum. The animals in that place were very well-trained. They didn't move a muscle when I walked through.

Of course, I chewed on many things – pillows, shoes, teddy bears, gloves and stuff. I got Lady's father's plaid Scottish cap one Thanksgiving. She repaired the pompom, and he learned to put his hat on higher ground. I've strewn lots of trash in my life – it's still a quick cure for boredom.

Labradors are generally late bloomers. Being large puppies for years suits our fun-loving personalities. But we're also smart and like to work, so the dog guides who receive lots of expert training early in their lives learn incredible skills and become extremely well-mannered in a relatively short time.

Just so you know, when real dog guides are not on duty, they sometimes act like puppies and steal sandwiches and get into trash, too.

2

Leader Dog School

On my first birthday, June 25, 1994, I received this birthday card! On the inside was printed:

*Give your puppy a birthday hug from all of us.
Please contact the school with your plans for
returning for formal training.*

And this hand-printed note was under that:

*We would like to schedule
return for early July.*

This was my call to duty. My marching orders. My *raison d'etre* at that time in my life. Mister and Lady knew this day would come.

I was just beginning to be enjoyable and mind some of my manners, and it was time to go. I was well-trained to get into a car and lie on the floor. Dog guides can't sit on seats in public transportation. I had never put my head out the window either because there's dust and dirt in the air that can damage a dog's eyes.

The day Mister and I left for the airport, I stepped in the back of his Thunderbird and for some reason, unknown even to me, I got on the seat and rested my head on the back window ledge.

Lady was standing in the driveway, bravely smiling and waving. I think I saw a tear roll down her cheek. When we started down the street, I got on the floor where I knew I should be.

I'd been in airports and on airplanes before, so not much was new there. As with my other flights, it was tough to get a long nap with the flight attendants petting me frequently. We rented a car in Detroit, and Mister drove about 30 miles north to Rochester and the Leader Dogs for the Blind headquarters.

I could have spent four days outside the building and a week in the front lobby - so many smells, so many dogs to meet by nose. I saw a couple dogs and heard others, Labradors I believe. I thought I was in for a barrel of fun.

Well, not exactly. A nice man took my leash, and we walked outside for 10 minutes. I heeled and stood still and sat on command. I was a model of good behavior so Mister would be pleased.

Then something strange happened. Mister left, and I was taken to a kennel and put in it with a few other dogs. I made friends with them right away. At bedtime, I barked for Mister and Lady and I missed them.

Over the next few days, I was examined by nice people. I went outside a little each day with some of my new housemates. This was a very big doghouse with space for about 300 dogs. I was hoping Mister would come and open all the kennel doors so we could play. Labradors are filled with playfulness.

But this was not a play place. This was a place for some serious business. I was not able to continue Leader Dog training because of bilateral hip dysplasia, and I had a small operation so I could not pass along this trait to new puppies.

During my short stay, however, I saw some of the training. To this day, I am very proud that I belonged to this elite dog population that becomes eyes for someone whose eyes don't work properly. It was a privilege to be associated with Leader Dogs, even if I would not grow up to serve as a dog guide.

Mister returned several days later, and we flew home. Lady was still standing in the driveway, and I wondered if she had been out there all week, waiting for me to come home. We were happy to be reunited, to be a pack again, each of us present and accounted for, ready to carry on with our innkeeping responsibilities.

3

My First Week

by Kent

One day I was in a kennel at Leader Dogs for the Blind in Rochester, Michigan, and the next day I was in a Ford Explorer with Solomon, Mister and Lady heading south. I tried to get in the front seat for most of the 580 miles. Solomon generously shared the two-thirds of the vehicle allotted to us, but I really wanted to be in front with my new people.

We stayed in a motel the first night, and I slept on the floor next to Mister. The second night we were at my new home, and they made me a simple bed of egg crate foam with a sheet on it. It is kitty-corner from Solomon's bed and about four feet from Mister and Lady's bed. I got on it, laid down and stayed there all night.

My first full day as junior innkeeper dog-in-training at Clay Corner Inn was a Thursday. Feelings of uncertainty about this new place and what was expected or acceptable washed over me, and I had a couple accidents. They handled me gently each time – one firm NO and a quick trip outside.

Once out there, we looked at each other. I think I was supposed to do something, but I didn't need to any more. After that we went outside lots of time each day, especially after my naps. When I took a pee, they became very happy, and I received lots of pets and hugs.

I threw up in the kitchen the first morning. Another quick trip outside, but this time I got a large, gentle hug and lots of sympathy. It never happened again.

They set up a crate in the office next to Solomon's and put soft stuff on the bottom. I've already wasted too much time in a kennel, and I would not go into it. No amount of coaxing would convince me to put even one paw inside there.

Later in the day, Solomon curled up in my crate – maybe to show me it was okay and to reinforce what they said about not closing the crate door. Perhaps some day I'll be comfortable with it, but now I'm afraid they will close the door and go away.

Every morning, I was hooked to a leash at the edge of the kitchen. I watched the breakfast preparations and sniffed lots of new smells. Mister and Lady walked in and out of the kitchen dozens of times, taking plates of food out, bringing empty plates back.

I walked around the public areas on my leash, seeing the people and letting them pet me. Lady asked me to sit and I did. Everyone commented on what a good dog I am for being just 2 years old.

By the end of this first week, I was allowed to be off my leash for short periods in the late afternoon and evening. It was fun being at the door to greet people and help Solomon with his public relations job. I also helped him with maintenance, specifically his Territorial Inspection Notwithstanding Kitty and Litter Evacuation (TINKLE) duties on the property. I followed him and copied everything he did.

Solomon is never on his leash in the inn. That's what I'm aspiring to – to be trusted to see the people, not touch the food, not go upstairs and be able to walk around without constant supervision.

I like it here very much. I like Mister and Lady and Solomon and the staff and the guests. I like my bed and my new food. I like walking and running on the Huckleberry Trail and in the woods next to the Virginia Tech stadium. Everything is wonderful - except the crate.

Kent

Like Solomon, I will always be proud to have been associated with Leader Dogs for the Blind. I have hip dysplasia in one hip, so I also could not become a dog guide for a blind person.

I am very fortunate that I can serve as junior innkeeper dog, making travelers feel welcome when they come to Clay Corner Inn. I'm also lucky that I can contribute one chapter to this book and go to some of the book signings. I hope they make a rubber stamp of my paw, too!

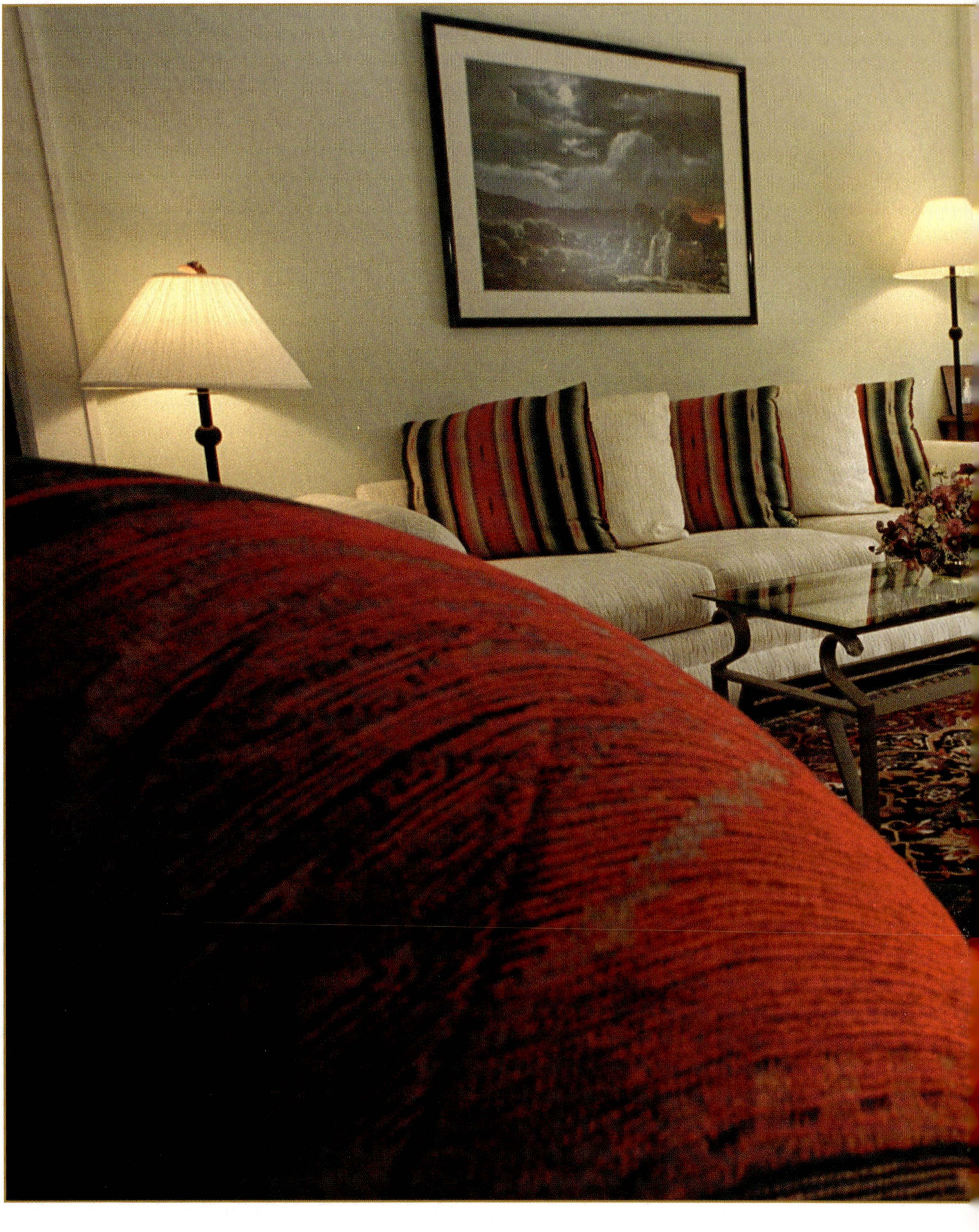

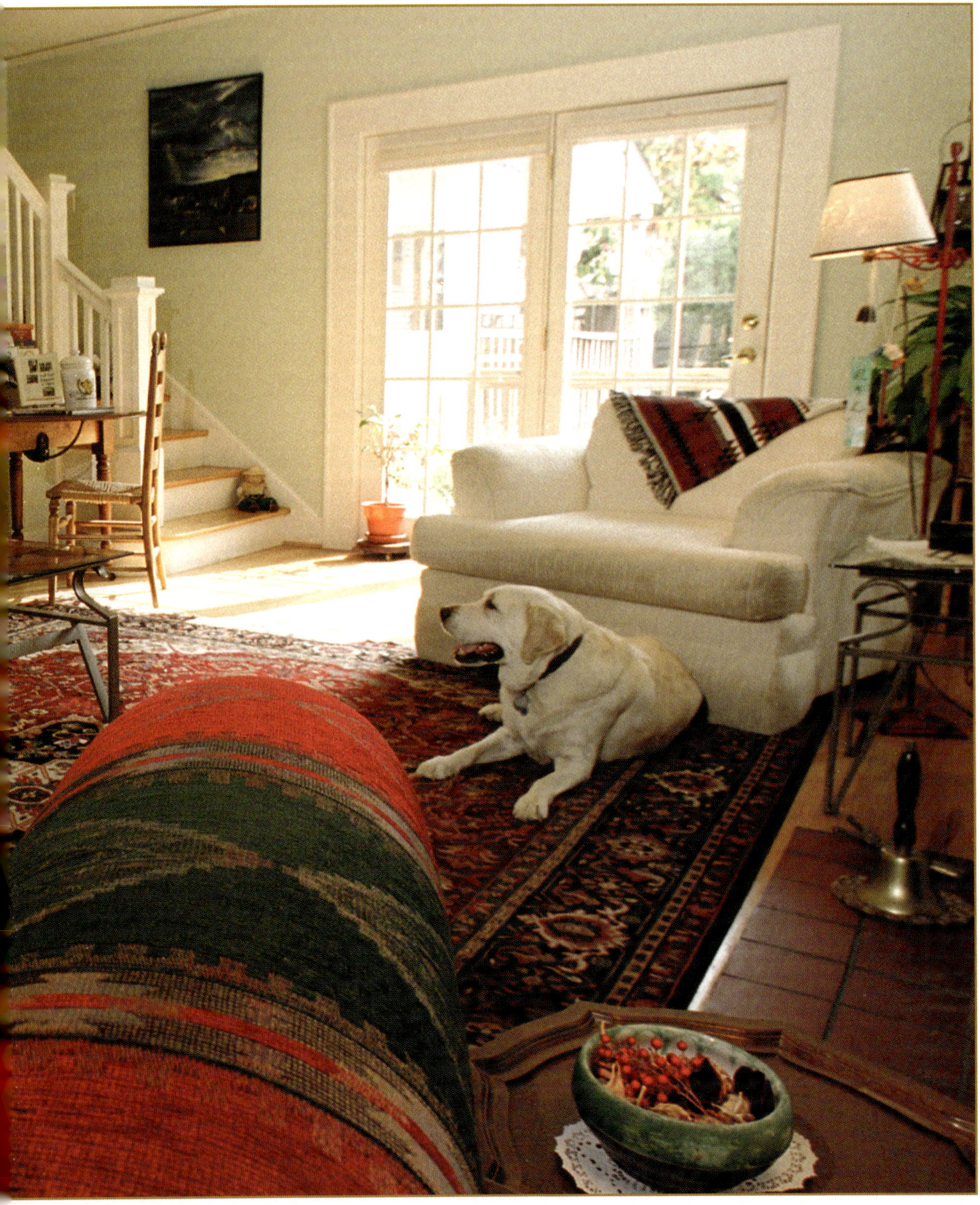

4

Business Overview

    This is a great business for dogs and people. Uh, make that very friendly dogs and friendly people. We - me and my passive, people-loving canine compatriots - are particularly well-suited because we like everyone without regard to size, hairdo, hearing aids, hometown, hauteur or the kind of car they drive. Innkeepers need to receive everyone with the same warmth and congeniality as we do.
    We dogs are fair in our treatment of guests. We sniff them all. I can tell right away if a person has a dog or, heaven forbid, a cat. If they spilled lunch on their clothes, I know it. I can tell you stories about their feet that you don't care to hear.
    People need many more skills than dogs to operate a B&B. Welcoming and entertaining guests, assuring squirrel-free and cat-free grounds, testing the swimming pool and some unsolicited maintenance and cleanup details here and there pretty much sums up my job description.
    Innkeepers, on the other hand, must possess a wide variety of skills starting with higher standards than dogs in the cleanliness department. They must know – or be quick learners – about cleansers and sanitation, linens, decorating, money management, public relations, advertising, personnel issues, taxes and licenses, marketing, food preparation, zoning laws, maintenance and repair, bookkeeping and accounting, computers and a host of other things.
    Suffice it to say that innkeepers are versatile, healthy, high-energy, multi-talented people who are comfortable serving others and enjoy staying at home. Key words in that previous sentence are "serving" and "staying." "Serving" others means that you may be treated like a service person occasionally, and this isn't

always compatible with one's ego. "Staying" can be overwhelming when cabin fever sets in during busy months and trips to the grocery and discount stores are the only outings for too many weeks.

The neat part for me is staying at home. When I cannot travel with Mister and Lady, I stay here, supervise whoever is innsitting, and carry on with my work. Those of you who own dogs already know that every trip into our own back yard or down the same street represents a new and interesting adventure.

The term "bed and breakfast" is pretty self-explanatory. However, let me explain further these two things. The "bed" part, obviously, refers to overnight lodging. Guest rooms stand at the ready - furnished, decorated, clean - absurdly clean if you ask me. They are rented by the night and cleaned for the next guest.

And "breakfast" is the morning meal served to guests. And here's the irony of it all. While the room takes less than an hour to clean, breakfast goes on all day - cooking, serving, cleaning up, planning, shopping, baking, emptying the dishwasher, ironing napkins, setting tables, prepping for the next morning and other necessary details.

Lady calls breakfast a "loss leader." It's much more time-consuming than the guest room, although it's the guest room that generates the revenue. Of course, it is our choice to offer a comprehensive, healthy, homemade breakfast buffet with a hot entrée every day. I like it because there are many possibilities for errant crumbs.

All in all, it's a good business for the right dogs and people. I like what I overhead one innkeeper tell Lady in the beginning:

Where else can you work that people come to your house, tell you how lovely it is, sleep in a guest room, compliment your decor, eat your food, tell you what a wonderful cook you are, and then give you money?

5

Business Plan

While I may not have much personal experience with business plans, I watch and listen to what's going on around me. This is, after all, a book about my observations.

Mister is a small business consultant and goodness knows I've lain around many a meeting with one floppy ear open. Lady writes articles on business subjects, so I catch information from her conversations as well.

It appears to me that the purpose of creating a business plan, unlike most business activities, does not rest with the result, but rather with the process. The goal of the work is not the finished, printed plan, but rather the thinking, projecting, planning, learning, considering trade-offs, juggling numbers, deciding how to handle details, creating policies and procedures and examining all facets of a prospective business, any kind of business.

Creating a business plan is a little like chasing a cat. Catching the cat is not really the objective. It's the chase that's important. The process. The action. Which most often ends for me at the bottom of a tree.

I was only 1 year old when they spent a few days and nights running numbers and tossing around ideas about buying this B&B. Now that I think of it, I don't believe I was mentioned in the plan. And look what an important team player I've turned out to be!

Going through the exercise of developing a business plan is the most important thing one can do for those involved and for the business because it answers the fundamental question: "Does this business make sense?"

Many people think because they have a head full of ideas and even the money to finance those ideas, and even a dog or two, they don't need a business plan. Faulty thinking, indeed, especially in the innkeeping business where the stakes can be very high and include, but are not limited to, financial investment – yours or someone else's – emotional and physical health, and loss of personal time and space. With the right attitude and perspective, however, along with a faithful dog or two, one can manage and enjoy success in this business.

One of the things in a business plan is a simple analysis of the competition, stressing "difference" over "better than." What makes your business different from similar enterprises? Why will someone choose one business instead of another? This also helps to define your market and establish the kind of image that will be portrayed.

The whole business plan should be written in an easy, concise manner which is neither wordy nor redundant. Photographs, biographies, drawings, dog photos, sample sales literature and other supporting material can be arranged in appendices.

Once all facets of the business have been analyzed and documented, one can communicate with integrity and confidence. With the plan in hand, or paw, one is prepared to entice and interest any number of people, including bankers and prospective employees and canine companions.

6

Mission Statement

It is the mission of Clay Corner Inn to provide safe, comfortable, clean lodging in a professional yet home-like setting with the amenities of a hotel and friendly atmosphere of a small inn.

We knew this all along, but documented it in writing six and a half years after entering the business and one week after reading *The Path* by Laurie Beth Jones. She believes that everyone should have a mission statement. I'm going to make one just for me and put it at the end of this chapter.

Jones also writes that few CEOs can recite their company's mission statement. Mister and Lady think that many of today's mission statements look like someone took a string of buzzwords, connected them with prepositions and conjunctions and threw in an occasional verb to make sentences.

According to Jones, a mission statement should meet three criteria: 1. No more than one sentence long. 2. Easily understood by a 12-year-old. 3. Able to be recited by memory [quickly].

Classic and simple mission statements include Abraham Lincoln's – *to preserve the Union*; Mother Teresa's – *to show mercy and compassion to the dying*; and Franklin D. Roosevelt's – *to end the Depression.*

Nelson Mandela lived and worked *to end apartheid*, while Joan of Arc's mission was *to free France*. The greatest mission statement of time was spoken by Jesus Christ and is recorded in the Bible (NIV), John 10:10: *I have come that they may have life*.

Dogs have many missions such as search and rescue, assisting the blind and handicapped, herding sheep, pulling sleds, sniffing for drugs, providing security, catching criminals, and being companions.

Those of us in the hospitality industry need to be well-mannered, considerate, non-biased, happy and agreeable. Working with the public can be challenging. Imagine my position dealing with a cat lover who strays on to the property for a night or two.

We have guests who are afraid of dogs and others who don't like dogs. I stay away from guests who are afraid. I remain in the office or kitchen so they will be comfortable when they're in the main house or having breakfast. I don't pay much attention to people who don't like dogs.

My mission is not to win people over to me and my canine compatriots. My mission is simply to offer a warm, happy welcome to everyone who enters the door. Hey, that's it – my mission statement: ☞☞☞☞☞☞☞☞☞

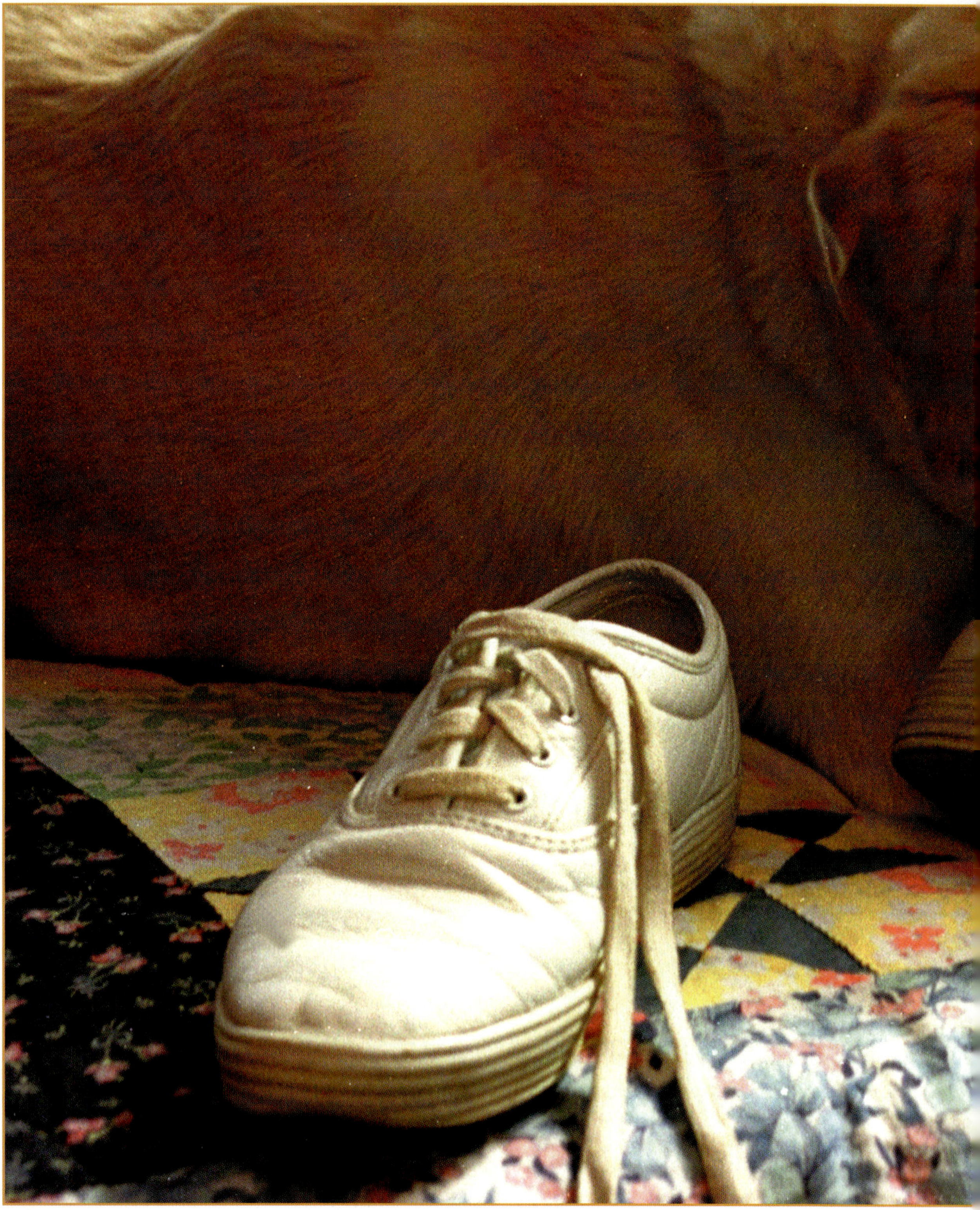

To welcome everyone with unconditional acceptance.

7

Innkeeper Quarters

Our bedroom over the office is not a big room. It's a rectangle about 8 feet by 14 feet with a little square on one side where two mismatched dressers face each other. There's about three feet between them and a window at the end. One is a tall, blond oak veneer bureau that matches the bedroom set in one of the guest rooms. The other is a short, dark walnut piece - a flea market find, I believe, that doesn't match anything. The handles aren't even the same.

There's a very nice treadmill next to the other window. I understand that most home exercise equipment accumulates dust, but not this one. Well, not often. I must tell you that the whole concept of a treadmill is lost on me when there's such excitement in the real world outside.

It is the only common interest I know of shared by humans and hamsters. Let me hasten to say that while I may not share that particular interest, I do admire the hamster for its innate ability to shred paper into such small pieces.

We also have a couple of odd bedside stands in our room, along with a wobbly lamp, a laundry hamper and a dining room chair.

Lady is going to fix up this room with new curtains, nice furniture, a headboard, floor lamp and a small easy chair. But no sooner does she say so, when she concedes that decorating expenses go to guest space first, and there's always something needed somewhere else that's more important.

Of course, as you may guess and you will certainly know after reading my version of what's going on around here, all the attention and expense that goes into decorating seems quite needless to me. I'd buy a boat or a convertible with the money they spend on linens and associated accoutrements.

Probably the best thing about our room is the lack of cleanser smell found everywhere else. Oh, we stock a veritable repertoire of cleansers, but Lady doesn't have time to keep it as spotless as guest rooms, so - for me, at least - it's more tolerable. Also, Mister's clothes just drop to the floor. He's not a person one would classify as a picker-upper. Standing just 2 feet 6 inches to the top of my head, I find life more interesting when there are lots of things on the floor.

Also, our room is our only private place on the entire property. One of the most frequently asked questions we get about being innkeepers concerns the lack of privacy. It's true, we don't have a lot of privacy. But that's the nature of the business, and it agrees with me, social animal that I am.

The heavy socialization, however, came as a bit of a surprise to Lady, and it was Mister who simplified this early on for her. She might lament that she wished the guests would finish breakfast so she could go to work.

"You are working," Mister gently chided. "This is your new job."

Innkeepers who renovate the family home into a bed and breakfast have a more difficult time with the transition from home to business. We bought our place as a business, so we don't have a home. We just live at the business.

Some innkeepers have an apartment for themselves. Others live in a house nearby. We have thought seriously about moving into the house behind the pool which has been rented since we bought it. There are pros and cons which get tossed around now and again, but for now, we live right in the main house.

We know innkeepers who have only a bedroom and do all the B&B paperwork and behind-the-scenes business in that one room. While we don't have the luxury of an apartment, we do have a wonderful office right below. And it's a short commute. Sixteen steps from "home" to work. All downhill.

31

8

Wake-up Call

We three - me, Mister Innkeeper and Lady Innkeeper - are asleep on our queen bed in our little room over the office when the morning alarms begin — a clock radio and battery-powered clock. The latter is a necessity anywhere the power goes out, which is basically anywhere in the world or wherever you are when you have a very important meeting early in the morning.

We shared a double bed for quite a while, but there just wasn't enough space for me to stretch without pushing on someone, so they bought us the larger bed. It works well, although I don't care for lining up parallel like sardines, as they would have it. I like flexibility depending on my mood, my dreams, the room temperature, where my pillow is and other factors.

Some readers may be astonished at this arrangement. Actually, no one is more surprised at having a dog on the bed than Lady herself, who had never allowed a dog on a bed before me. But I'll have you know that many great folks in history purportedly slept with their dogs – Ramses the Great, Peter the Great, Frederick the Great, to name a few.

Somewhere around 50 percent of American dog owners share bed space with a dog, maybe two or three (dogs). And there's a practical side to such an arrangement - namely, body heat. I've heard that the Australian rock group Three Dog Night is a reference to some very cold nights in the Outback.

Some time around 6:15 a.m. and occasionally as late as 7:45 the beeping begins and the radio starts blaring. You'd think they were hard of hearing. On the other hand, this is not the kind of business where you ever want to oversleep. It's never happened to us - not yet.

Lady arises and takes a shower and heads downstairs. When Mister moves to the bathroom, I can stretch out all over the place. I don't get up until absolutely necessary.

Occasionally the order is reversed with Mister getting up first and Lady second. This disrupts my final bed rest because she wants to tidy up the bed before going downstairs. She softly says "off" to me, and I move one paw toward the edge of the mattress to see if she's serious.

She is the disciplinarian of our pack, so it's pretty likely that she'll follow through on a command. But I give her my sleepy sad-brown-eyed-look anyway. She returns it with an exasperated please-get-off-the-bed look and repeats "off," just barely above a whisper. I lumber down.

That Lady speaks softly to me is often noticed. And if you know anything about dogs, you know that our sense of hearing is quite acute. Thus, it doesn't make any sense to shout at a dog. So why do people do it? Far be it from me to try to explain any aspect of human behavior, but here's what Lady says when people ask.

"Dogs have no trouble hearing. They have trouble with attention. If a dog is not paying attention to you, forget it. If you have the dog's attention, you will be heard without raising your voice." Getting our attention is the tricky part.

Anyway, when the last person goes down, I stretch my legs and follow - prepared to begin another innkeeper dog day.

9

The Kitchen

 People are always surprised that our kitchen is so small – working floor space is about 6 feet by 11 feet not including the counters, cupboards, stove, sink and refrigerator. The kitchen is a good place to hang out, the heart of the home I believe they say.
 It's also a good place to investigate the trash. You know the adage: *someone's trash may be your treasure*. I embrace that train of thought frequently. They think as I get older, I won't do this. Sometimes they seem a little vague about what being a Labrador means with regard to food. I am their first purebred Labrador retriever, so perhaps they are simply s—l—o—w l—e—a—r—n—e—r—s. Seven plus years and they still seem astonished when they find me searching through the trash for my treasure.
 Mister wants to put in a commercial kitchen, and Lady would love it. Like boats, convertibles and roofs, commercial kitchens are quite expensive. We have all new roofs on our buildings, which explains why we don't have a boat or convertible, and may or may not be getting a commercial kitchen.
 The size of the kitchen doesn't bother Lady. "It keeps us efficient," she quips. It's true. We can keep the buffet replenished and serve more than 30 people a full breakfast entrée out of here and still have vacant counter space. Sure, it gets a little crazy, but we can do it.
 We operate with one regular oven and stove, one basic refrigerator, everyday double sinks, a commercial garbage disposal, an average dishwasher, four coffeemakers, a large mixer and an electric grill.
 There's also a microwave oven, four-slice toaster and assorted mixing bowls

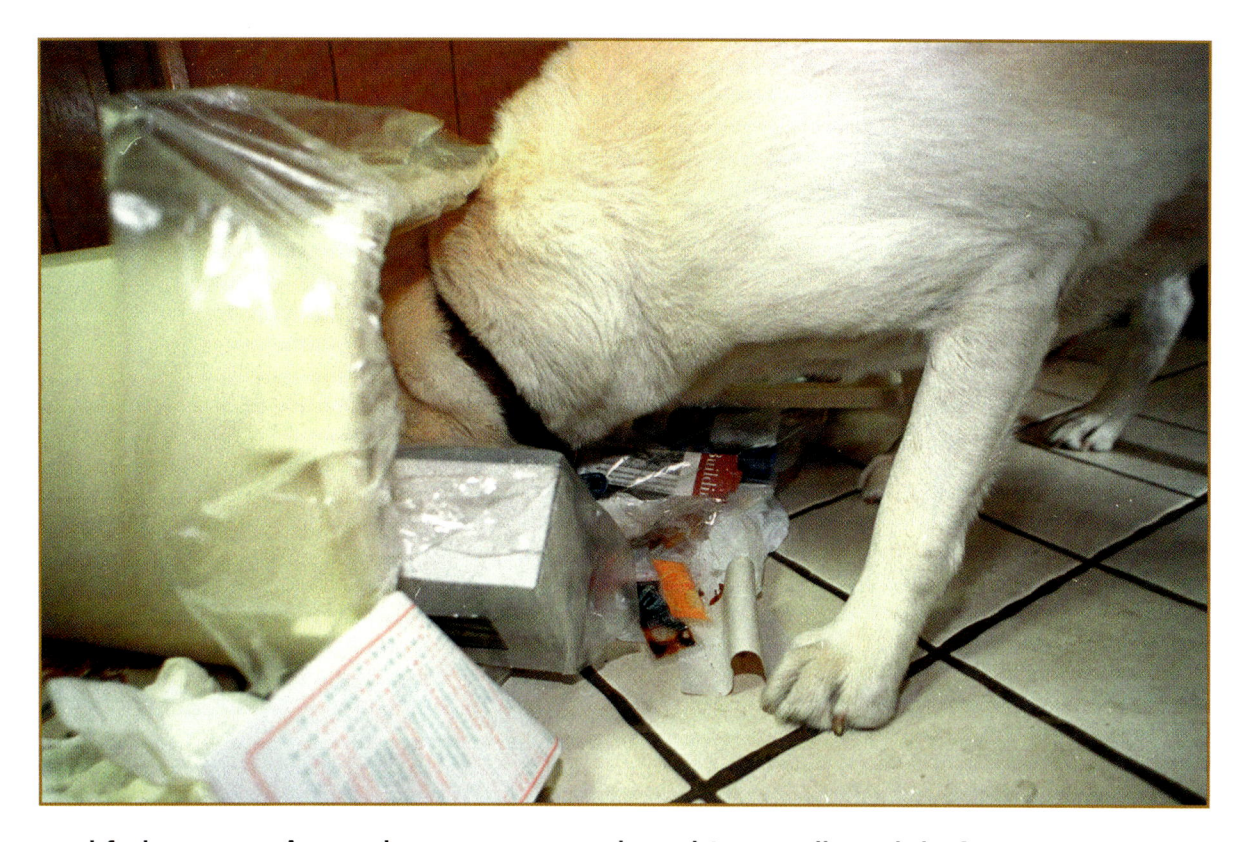

and frying pans. A couple years ago we bought a small, upright freezer so we can stockpile juice and breakfast meat. Nothing elaborate here.

There's a TV set on a turntable. We can turn it toward the kitchen or 180 degrees around to the little table at the end of the kitchen, next to windows that overlook the covered deck.

When Lady's mother came during the first year of business, she exclaimed, "Oh, how cute! This must be where you sit and have breakfast every morning!"

Not exactly, Betty. Mister and Lady don't actually SIT and HAVE breakfast most mornings. That's what the guests do.

But yes, if they were to sit and have breakfast, this would be the place. There is one hard and fast observation about this business that I'll share with you right now.

If Mister or Lady have hot food and sit down in front of it, the telephone or doorbell will ring or a guest will appear out of nowhere for something complicated. This has been proved day after day, week after week, month after month, year after year.

The only time I draw the line on greeting guests is when I am eating. I do not like to break my concentration, and what if someone took my food away when I wasn't looking? Not worth the chance. It doesn't always take three of us to connect with a guest who needs something, so I defer to others when there's food in my dish – or anywhere else within my reach.

10

Serving Breakfast

    During the week, breakfast is served at Clay Corner Inn between 7:30 and 9 a.m. and on weekends between 8:30 and 10 a.m. We go down about 30 minutes earlier to turn on the lights and the music, set up the buffet, cut fruit, load coffeepots, start the grill and get the newspaper.
    I have been encouraged to fetch the newspaper, and I take every step very seriously. Before I ever get to the paper, I am compelled to check shrubbery, tree trunks, the lamp post, the mail box post, the edge of the steps, a couple of small boxwood plants near the street, blades of grass - things no one else thinks of investigating for trespassers.
    I have watched this routine enough to know that the newspaper is taken out of its rubber band or plastic wrapper and separated by sections. So I remove any wrapper with my teeth, in the yard somewhere so it doesn't clutter the living room. I also separate the sections.
    Well, Mister and Lady get impatient with the time it takes for me to return with the newspaper, or parts of it, and I don't always get the sections exactly right. It's simply easier to let them get it.
    Every day we have a buffet and a hot entrée option. We make our own cereals, and offer two kinds each day, along with fresh fruit, yogurt, juice, coffee, tea, hot chocolate and homemade muffins, scones or coffeecake.
    One doesn't need to be a gourmet cook to make a good breakfast. Our daily hot entrée varies between French toast and pancakes with breakfast meat, eggs, baked oatmeal, quiche and other items - things made fresh and mostly on the plain side for universal appeal and good nutrition.

Lady often jokes that one only needs about four recipes and four outfits in this business - the people keep changing.

If we have more than 12 breakfast guests — and we serve up to 32 — an employee is scheduled and Mister serves as back-up for whatever is needed. I chip in with my social skills and occasional cleanup activities.

Portion sizes are modest and attractively arranged with some sort of garnish. Of course, it practically goes without saying that the canine population is not nearly so particular about the aesthetics of food on a plate. We don't, as the saying goes, "eat with our eyes." If anything, we eat with our noses.

For that matter, we don't even require the plate. Especially not these flimsy china ones which have been known to break under the slightest paw pressure or after a quick trip to the floor.

I've dutifully tried all the breakfast morsels when opportunities to do so were present. My favorite breakfast food is the meat, but I don't get it very often. Lady thinks that 96 pounds is heavy enough for a 24-inch high Labrador, measured at the shoulders.

Unbeknown to Lady, there are a few regular guests who slip me some tidbit during breakfast. I can identify them, but it's probably in my best interest, and perhaps theirs, not to reveal names or faces.

Anyway, I stick close to them and we both watch for Lady to disappear to the kitchen. She has said that the guests are harder to train than me. *Au contraire*, I find them to be quick learners for my purposes.

11

Breakfast Clean-Up

I've never gone hungry in my life. And I'm not hungry when cleanup time rolls around. So what's the attraction? Could be as simple as the forbidden fruit. I'm not supposed to have muffins and butter, and that alone makes them appealing. Taste is also a factor, and all our baked goods are made here, and they are delicious.

I am very fast at stealing these things. And I need to be - for a couple of reasons. If I get caught part way through cleaning up, I may lose whatever I have not yet consumed. Also, being fast and efficient is part of the *modus operandi* of innkeeping. There is so much work to do every day that speed and efficiency are paramount to accomplish the most in the time allotted - which is only 16 or so of the available 24 hours.

Here's the typical cleanup scenario. I am feigning pure relaxation on the living room rug, from where I can see who is coming and going. I am mostly interested in who's going. Once guests are about three feet from their table and there are no other guests in the room, it's time for action. I sniff and evaluate tabletop possibilities from the smells. I rise slightly on my back legs to check my suspicions visually.

When my eyes confirm what my nose detected, I move very fast. I gently lift a muffin basket or a little butter dish and hop right down: three to four seconds flat. They do not like me eating at the table, I know.

The muffin baskets are excellent because the bounty is more plentiful than say a tablespoon of butter, and the basket makes much less noise than a glass dish rattling between my teeth and the floor. I gently, but still very quickly, unpack the basket, separating the muffins from the napkin and, in the process, the napkin from the basket (without tearing or damaging either basket, napkin or muffin, I might add).

At this point, the scene can take any number of turns depending on guests checking out, the telephone ringing, how many dishes are piled in the sink, people engaging the innkeepers and staff in conversation, and so on. If things are busy, I can follow through entirely on my cleanup and finish all the edible portions of what I have retrieved. Remember, I'm a retriever.

If things are relatively calm, and my work is discovered before I am finished, I will receive at the very least an angry barrage of words. Not a speck of praise for my cleanup efforts.

Mister will come right over and take a muffin out of my mouth. Lady doesn't dare, and she tells her staff to leave me alone, too. That's because I bit her once. I shouldn't have, but you haven't tried our harvest muffins - mmmmmmm. They were too good to let go, and she wouldn't have used the ones on the floor anyway. I know I hurt her feelings and her finger, and I was sorry.

Fortunately, Lady has the precious dog trait of quick to forgive, and all was forgiven before sunset. I don't think anyone – dogs or people – should go to bed angry.

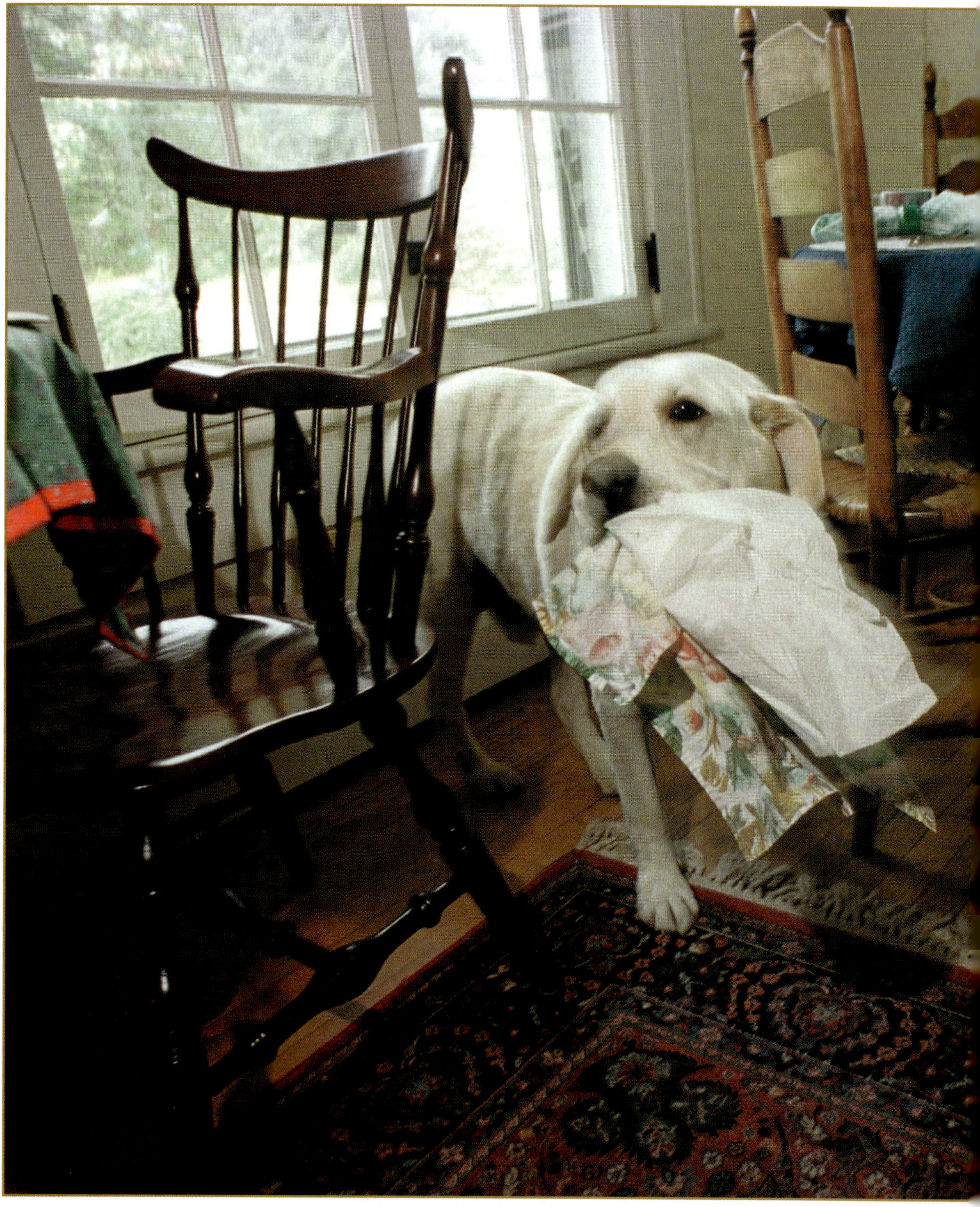

While I am not supposed to take things from the table tops, there are no restrictions on floor crumbs. I can have all of those, but they are very, very small and, for the most part, unsatisfying.

For their part, innkeepers and staff clear the tables, load the dishwasher, wash some dishes, put away buffet food, wipe counters, change table linens and, at the very end of breakfast time, they add water to the left-over coffee and set the pot(s) on the counter to cool.

Those of you who read the introduction know that Mister and Lady do not drink coffee. Neither do I. So the extra coffee is diluted, cooled, then given to the outdoor flower baskets or indoor plants. They like it, the plants do. It's not wasted, and we all feel better for having some use for old coffee.

> *Stealing muffins or bacon, jumping in a guest bed, walking in the guest room shower, swimming, rearranging newspaper pages – all these things bring me closer to the guests. By understanding what the guests experience, I feel that I can better serve them, even if it involves serving myself in the process.*

12

Cooking & Baking

I like to be around cooking and baking. My active participation is pretty much limited to snarfing up a morsel that makes its way to the floor, or stealing whatever I can from a countertop. My passive participation is just a support role of being good company, being a pet for the moment.

Our cooking activities are very easy because we serve breakfast during 90 minutes each morning. Fancy stuff like soufflés and timed-to-the-minute gourmet entrées would not be practical because we don't know when guests are coming. Another case for simplicity is universal appeal. We have guests from all over the world, and we find that plain food is most appealing to most of the people.

So we stick to pancakes, waffles, French toast, eggs Benedict, Philly eggs (scrambled eggs with cream cheese), baked oatmeal, quiche and a few baked egg and cheese dishes. We usually have bacon, sausage or ham with breakfast – and these are the most interesting items to me.

I get two chances at bacon because we prepare it the day before. You can try this at home. Line a cookie sheet with aluminum foil then place a cookie rack on it. Put bacon strips on the cookie rack. It doesn't need to be turned over, although we turn the cookie sheets around and change shelves half-way through. Bake for about 20-25 minutes at 350 degrees. In the morning, it can be heated in the microwave for about 10 seconds per slice.

We can cook 5 pounds in less than hour. Of course, how much we have to serve in the morning depends on how closely it was watched and how much I got. The truth is: I rarely get bacon, except when I had to take some antibiotics. Then I got two "legal" pieces a day with pills inside. I knew the pills were there, but who's going to quibble about what's inside the bacon?

Spiral sliced ham is a great invention, and we put it in a warm glaze that Mister makes. I can take it with or without the glaze. Our sausage is hand-pattied and fried on both sides, then placed in a pan of water to keep it hot and moist. You can try this at home, too.

There's a great advantage in having a few special appliances beyond the common toaster. We have electric egg poachers that click off when eggs are perfect for the eggs Benedict, and fancy-shaped waffle irons that chirp when ready for batter and chirp again when the batter is fully waffled and ready to serve. It doesn't get much easier than that.

When we first bought the B&B, Lady was pretty excited about having fresh-from-the-oven muffins each morning – the aroma of baking filling the morning air – a warm, fuzzy kind of nostalgic thing. Well, that didn't last.

As Clay Corner Inn grew in size and popularity, so did the volume of work in the morning to prepare breakfast. Flitting about the kitchen in an old-fashioned apron, humming and making muffins from scratch just couldn't be done. Nostalgia was replaced by practicality. So we bake most days of the week in the afternoon for the next morning.

There's no great secret to good baking. Muffin and cookie doughs are better mixed by hand. Eggs should be room temperature. Butter and cream taste better than margarine and milk. Dry buttermilk mix (mixed appropriately with water) works as well as real buttermilk.

Our convection oven blows around the dough too much, and muffins and coffeecakes come out skewed in height. Another short-lived great idea - this convection oven. Commercial ones are probably fine, but ours is a basic issue oven from the Sears appliance department.

We make muffins and scones, round coffeecakes and square ones, biscuits, breads and English muffin loaves. So much variety.

Need I point out one more time that it's people driving this business and making it more complicated than dogs would ever do? Labrador retrievers are not particular about such things as the shape of a muffin. Appearance and variety are way down on the list of priorities about food.

We would be fine, really fine, with the same flavor of coffeecake or the same form of pork every morning. We are truly easy to please in the food department. Just take me for a walk near the stadium after a Virginia Tech football game for a phenomenal stroll through *terra firma's* smorgasbord.

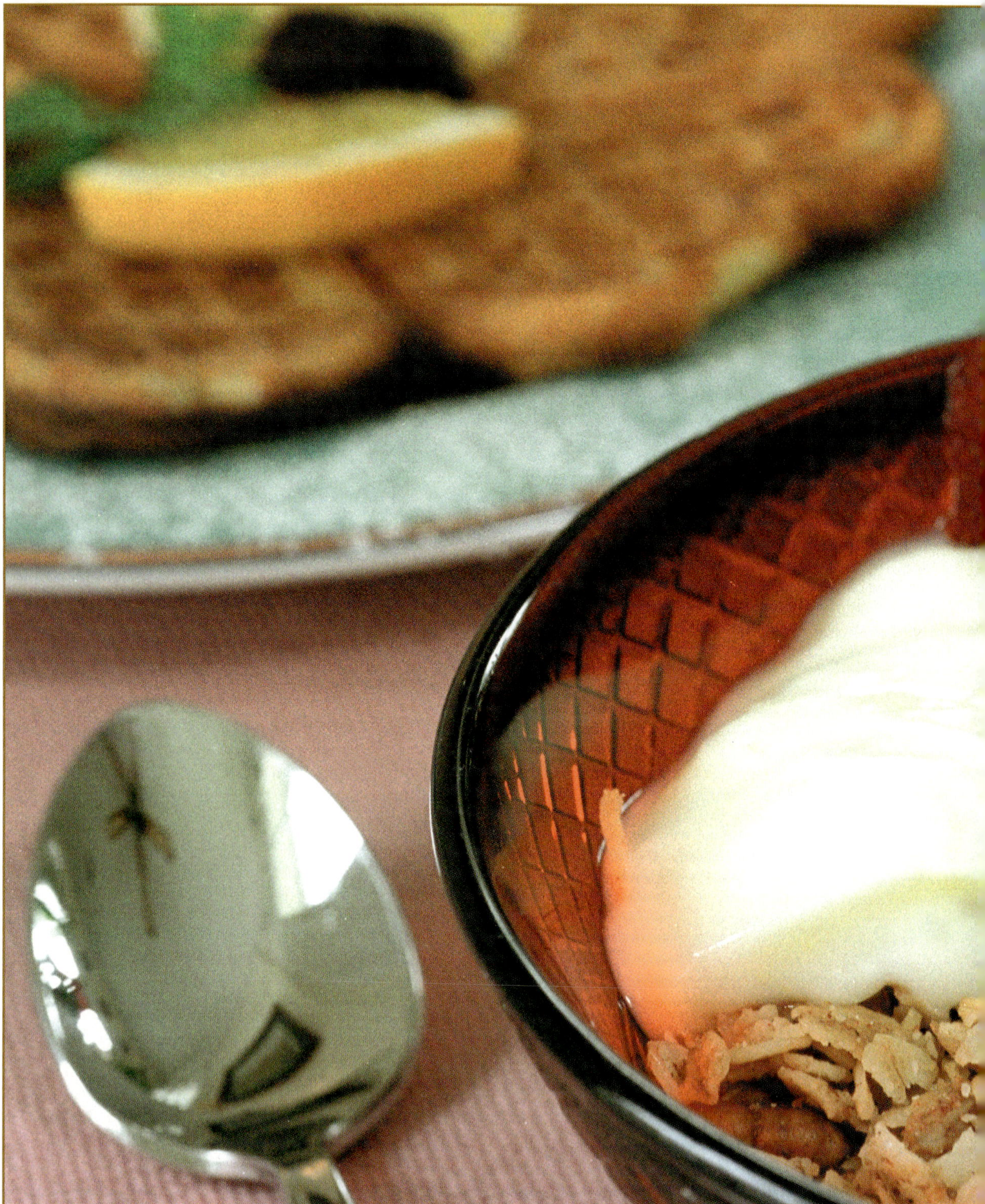

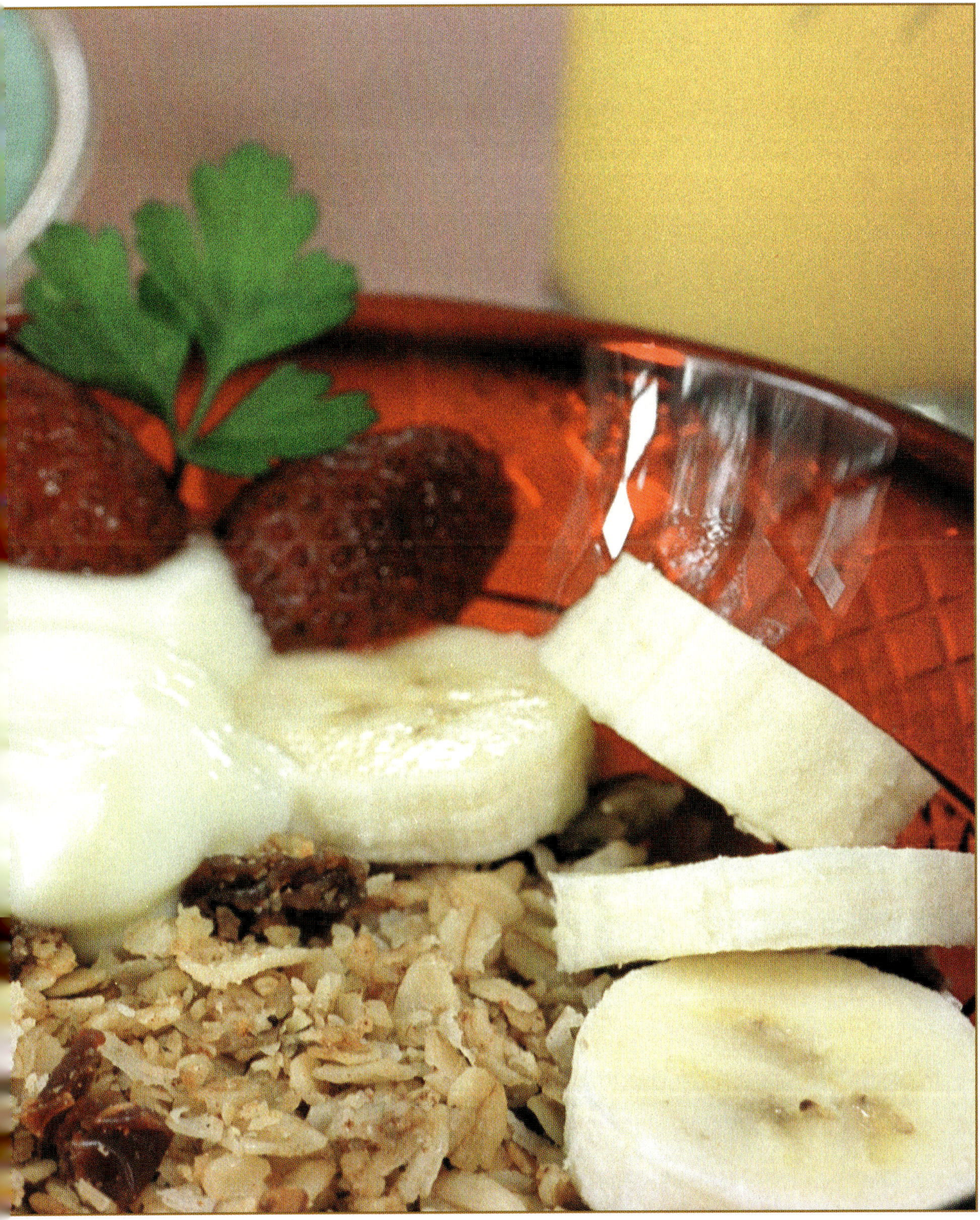

13

Recipes

There are many recipes and entire cookbooks just for dogs. But you know without being told that most of these are really for people. The same reason there are so many dog products for sale. It's really for the people, not the dogs.

We don't care about the color of our collars, the shape of our treats, the style of our dish or if our bed has our name embroidered on it. We can't even read.

But people – different ball of wax altogether. Picky, picky, picky – no one more so than Lady. She could be the Picky Queen of the Universe. And recipes are just another testament to the fact. They are followed precisely to create the same product every time.

I say throw a few things together, add lots of meat, scramble, bake if you wish, and eat heartily, as if there were no tomorrow. "Eating heartily" is actually an understatement of my breed's dining manner. Our slogan could be INgesting Heartily Assures Labrador Energy (INHALE).

The Clay Corner Inn orange date granola and dried cranberry meusli cereals were developed by Lady and former assistant innkeeper Robyn Furey. I cannot publish those, but I'll pass along some of the recipes that are very popular with guests. And with me, of course.

Baked oatmeal
Tastes like a crumbled oatmeal cookie, great winter dish, simple to prepare and serve, can be mixed and put into greased loaf pans, refrigerated overnight and baked in the morning. Also freezes well after baking. Can be doubled, tripled and quadrupled. Yield: 1 loaf

2 cups quick oats
1/4 cup melted margarine
1/2 cup brown sugar
3/4 cup milk
1 egg
1 tsp. baking powder
1 tsp. cinnamon
1/4 tsp. salt

(Optional: nuts, raisins, currants)
Mix dry stuff, then add margarine, milk and egg. Stir well. Put in greased loaf pan. Bake 25 minutes at 350.

Sour Cream Coffeecake
Serve in the morning for coffeecake; top with whipped cream and serve in the evening for dessert. Yield: 1 Bundt cake

2 cups flour
1 tsp. baking powder
1/2 tsp. baking soda
1/2 tsp. salt
1 cup butter
1 1/4 cups sugar
2 eggs
1 tsp. vanilla
1 cup sour cream

3 Tbl. Sugar
1 1/2 tsp. cinnamon
1/4 cup chopped walnuts

Mix first four dry ingredients; set aside. Blend butter and sugar with mixer; add eggs and vanilla. Add flour mixture alternately with sour cream, beating just until combined after each addition. Spread half the batter in greased Bundt pan. Sprinkle with sugar, cinnamon, nut mixture. Spread remaining batter on top. Bake at 350 about 45 minutes. Looks nice sprinkled with sifted powdered sugar.

Gingersnaps
Clay Corner Inn cookie of choice.
Yield: 3 dozen or so

1 1/2 cups shortening
2 cups sugar
1/2 cup dark molasses
2 eggs
4 cups flour
4 tsp. baking soda
1/2 tsp. salt
2 tsp. cinnamon
2 tsp. ginger
2 tsp. cloves

Mix shortening and sugar, add molasses and eggs. Then add and mix dry ingredients. If you use a mixer, blend only on low speed. Refrigerate dough for an hour or more. Shape in balls, flatten slightly, dip one side in sugar. Place sugar side up on ungreased cookie sheet. Bake for 13 minutes at 375.

Lemon Rosemary Coffeecake
Wonderfully moist and tasty. Yield: 3 round coffeecakes

3 3/4 cups flour
2 cups sugar

3/8 tsp. salt

Combine flour, sugar and salt in bowl and add 3/4 cup chilled butter (cut in small pieces) until mixture resembles coarse meal. Reserve 1 1/2 cups for topping.

Mix remaining flour mixture with:

3/4 tsp. dried rosemary
1 1/2 tsp. baking powder
3/4 tsp. baking soda
1 cup buttermilk
6 tablespoons lemon juice
3 eggs

Beat on medium speed until blended. Spoon batter into three 8" round pans coated with cooking spray. Combine reserved flour mixture with 6 tsp. grated lemon rind and 2 1/4 tsp water. Stir with fork, then sprinkle over coffeecakes. Bake at 350 for 30 minutes. Cool. Freezes well.

Nutmeg Muffins
Crunchy top, wonderful texture and taste. Mix all by hand. Yield: 12 muffins

Mix first three ingredients, reserve 3/4 cup for topping.

2 cups flour
1 1/2 cups light brown sugar
3/4 cup margarine, melted

Add and combine:

1 cup flour
2 tsp. baking powder
2 tsp. nutmeg
1/2 tsp. baking soda
1/2 tsp. salt

Gently stir in:

1 cup buttermilk
2 eggs

Spoon muffin tins half full, sprinkle with topping; bake in pre-heated oven at 350 for around 20 minutes.

Scottish Oatmeal Scones
Not the real cream scones of Scotland, but a close second when served warm with raspberry or seedless strawberry jam. Yield: 16 scones

2 1/2 cups flour
2/3 cup sugar
4 tsp. baking powder
1 tsp. salt
1/2 cup shortening
1/2 cup margarine, softened
2 cups quick oats
2/3 cup milk

Mix flour, sugar, baking powder and salt. Cut in shortening and margarine mixing with fork until it resembles coarse crumbs. Mix in oats. Add milk and stir just until dry ingredients are moistened.

Put half the dough on floured surface and knead just 6-7 times. Pat in circle about 3/4 – inch thick. Cut in pie wedges, place on ungreased cookie sheet, bake at 375 about 12 minutes, until very lightly browned on edges.

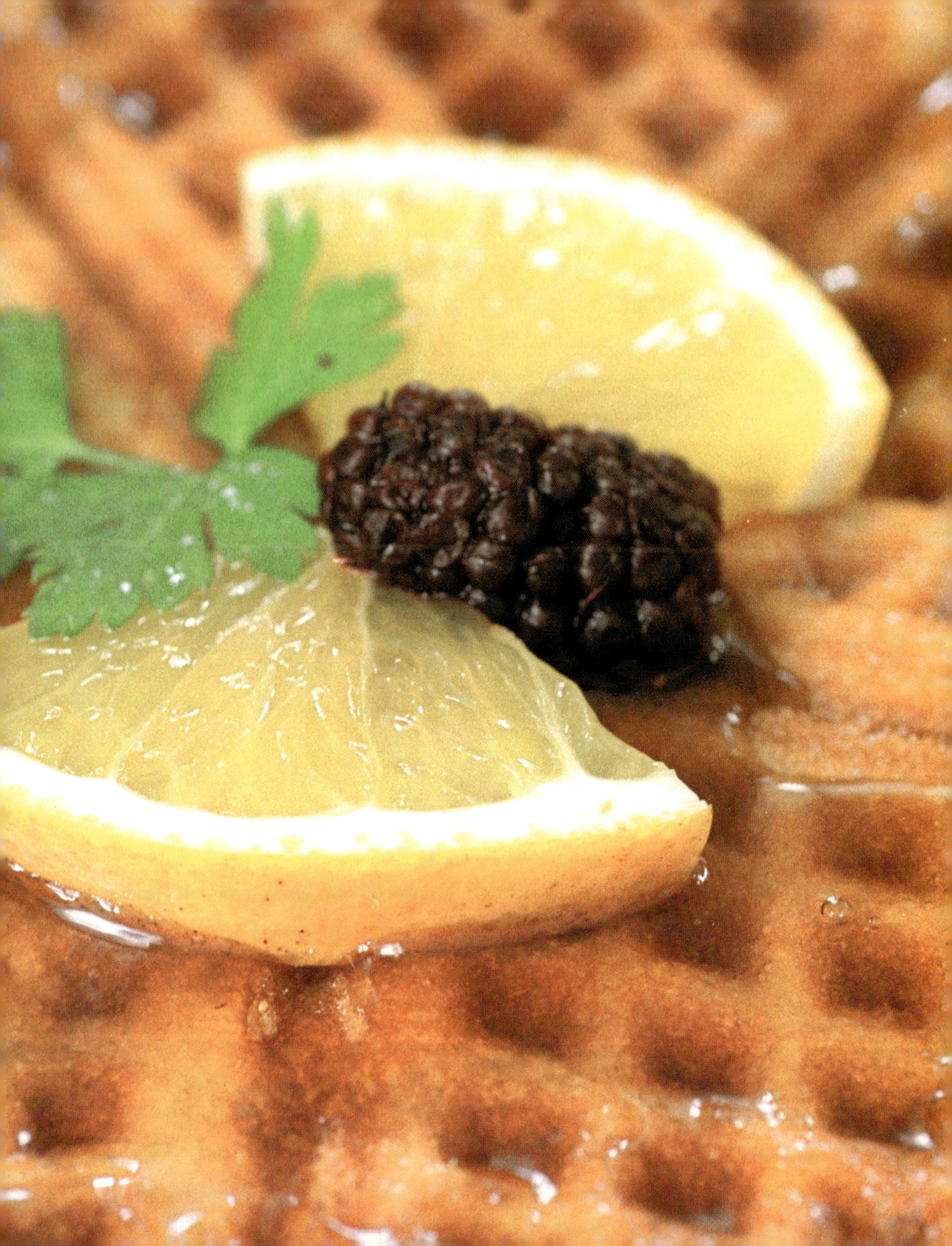

14

The Guest Room

I'm not allowed to spend much time in our guest rooms, but if I do get into one, I would like to get on the bed. You may think this is because I like something soft, but it's really because I like to be up high to see better what's going on around me.

The guest room, as you can figure out, is the nucleus of our business - our *raison d'etre*, if you will. As such, careful planning has gone into creating guest rooms that are comfortable, functional, attractive and very clean.

The bed is the centerpiece, and ours are high-quality queen or king box spring and mattress, firm but also quilted or topped with egg carton foam. Bear in mind that while one can't please all the people, innkeepers have no trouble with canine guests about the firmness of the bed.

Same with pillows, although personally I steer away from the firm ones. Medium firmness is the best bet. Each bed has four pillows because some people like to read or watch TV in bed. Some dogs like lots of pillows, too.

Lady has a headboard on every bed to protect the wall, look more attractive and allow some creative angle positioning of the bed. We prefer comforters and dust ruffles, and those dust ruffles must be straight at the bottom just a hair - or a fur - off the floor. Lady goes ballistic when she sees crooked dust ruffles - looks sloppy, she says. Picky, picky, I say.

Of course, there's a dresser, easy chair, writing table and chair, good lighting at chairs and on each side of the bed. There's a tendency to think of a writing table for business travelers, but lots of people will use a table for writing letters and post cards, untangling a necklace or putting on nail polish. Dogs like to lie under tables for security and safety from clumsy feet.

There's a clock radio in every room at Clay Corner Inn. Not everyone has a travel clock (or as in our case, can find it before a trip - better edit this out - oops!). Mister and Lady rarely remember to wear a watch. We've had to go buy a clock more than once, or go to the car to find out the time. This annoys them. (One would think one of them might remember to wear a watch. Hmmmmmm.)

The 5-inch by 7-inch frame on each dresser displays basic information like check-in and check-out times, breakfast hours, where to find soda, and swimming pool or hot tub information. It should remind guests that there are DOG TREATS IN THE WHITE CERAMIC CONTAINER ON THE REGISTRATION TABLE WITH THE PICTURE OF THE LABRADOR AND LATIN WORDS: CANIS EATEMIS ANTHINGIS.

Each room has a notebook of information which includes the property's history, amenities, a town map, restaurants, attractions and events, brochures, etc. Of course, I'd throw in best parks for dogs, nearby streams and ponds, location of cats to chase, most likely rabbit field, good trash cans - everything except perhaps where the llamas live (see Vacation chapter).

The guest rooms have carpeting or rugs one can't trip over, drapes and/or shades that close well, a closet or armoire with wood or plastic hangers including clip hangers for skirts and slacks, a fly swatter, iron and ironing board, luggage rack, flashlight and Bible.

Books and magazines are a nice touch. *Old Yeller, Lassie, Memoirs of a Yellow Dog, My Dog Skip* and *A Dog's Life* are classics. Magazines like *Dog Fancy* and *Dog World* would be my choices.

Door knob and deadbolt locks are necessary in this uncertain world, but for us dogs, a simple flap or curtain will suffice. You can see clearly now, I hope, that it's people who make innkeeping the monumental amount of work that it is. Not dogs.

15

Furniture

    I like furniture, some better than others. I like beds the most because they're spacious and easy to get on. They are not made for any kind of walking around – too soft and unwieldy underfoot, uh, underpaw, that is – but a bed is neatly form-fitting and usually comes with pillows.

    Couches are my second favorite piece of furniture, although I haven't been on too many. Tables that hold food are good. Sturdy chairs next to tables that hold food are very good, if you catch my drift.

    Big easy chairs are suitable for some dogs. Of course, some dogs are so small that little easy chairs are fine. Cats seem to have much more liberty with getting on furniture than dogs. Cats just have more liberties altogether. Take, for example, the dinner party of yesteryear.

    A long time ago, Lady's mother, Betty Brown, was having a dinner party. The finest linens were set, some of the china was in place, and she went to dress for the occasion. Upon her return, she and Lady found the house cat at the time, a pretty, brindle feline named Prudence, curled in a ball, feigning sound sleep on the hors-d'oeuvres table just a whisker from the punch bowl.

    They scooped the cat gently in their hands, trying not to disturb him or his circular body arrangement, and gently laid him on an easy chair, petted his head, cooed a little and left him there. Do you have any idea what might befall a dog that curled up on the finest linens next to the punch bowl moments before the guests' arrival? I can promise you that a Lab wouldn't be scooped up so lovingly and merely transplanted in its curled-up manner. No way.

    And I would love to know who is responsible for designing doghouses so small that furniture is not even an interior option. Oh, humans think they're very clever if they put real shingles on the top, a rug on the floor and a window. I read somewhere about a doghouse that was air-conditioned. Nice folks, considering that we wear our coats all year, and summer days can be toasty.

Furniture provides a dog with options – something to chew on during dull times, something on which to sit or take a nap, something to tip over and play with, something to investigate – like what's inside or underneath a cushion.

The furniture at the B&B is nice enough. I'm not allowed on any of it. Lady spends the most money on beds. A headboard keeps pillows from falling on the floor. Personally, I like pillows on the floor just as much as on the bed. I'm fond of simple square pillows I can carry or full-size ones for sleeping.

There are so many requirements in the people world that it's lucky there's room to walk in a B&B guest room. Our rooms average about 15 feet square, and each one must have a king or queen bed, one or two night stands, an easy chair, a dresser, a writing table and chair, television set and lamps and assorted small things. Not much space left over.

Furniture is expensive, but Lady and Mister are always upgrading, replacing and improving some furniture or another. We went to North Carolina one time, visiting all the furniture outlets in and around Hickory – famous for their furniture, they are.

Everything was above our budget (which could say something about the budget). We came back with one easy chair – a swivel rocker thing that is far too unpredictable for me to use. Then Lady drove to the next town and bought precisely what she wanted for love seats at Grand Home Furnishings. She likes their furniture as much as their flexible payment plan.

If I make a little money on this book, I think I'll buy some luxurious furniture for my office crate – a nice mattress with a soft, sheepskin cover and lots of squishy pillows. And maybe my own loveseat.

16

Decorating

We have a separate expense category for decorating. Do you want to know what it was last year?? Let's see, I double click on Quick Books Pro and then on some report thing – I'll get it.

Oh, my – it's four digits and the first one doesn't begin with number one. That's all I can tell you. It wouldn't buy a convertible or a boat, but it could support a nice two-room doghouse.

Don't get me wrong. Some decorating is okay. I'm not adverse to a picture on the wall here and there, straight or otherwise, cheap or expensive, watercolor or oil or print. I'm not much for landscapes or still life, but a good dog portrait can be appealing. And expensive. You know, the whole dog painting thing started with a dog-loving queen.

It seems that when Victoria was 17 years old, she received a portrait of her spaniel, Dash, as a present from one Duchess of Kent. The year was 1836, and after little Vicky became queen the following year, she commissioned many dog portraits.

Today one can pay over $100,000 for a dog portrait. I could buy a boat AND a convertible with that kind or money. I could buy a boat AND a convertible AND a really big doghouse with the $557,500 that was paid in 1989 for a painting of a Newfoundland hound named Neptune.

I understand the nature of humans enough to know that visual appeal is important. Personally, I'm much more partial to smell. It's color-coordination that baffles me.

I'm cream color, I know that, but it's just a variation of white. Do you know how many variations of white there are? At Valley Paint and Decorating, our Benjamin Moore paint store, owner Duane Mills showed me hundreds of colors and dozens of shades of white. I was much more interested in the treat he was holding behind everything to get me in the photo than in those small specks of color.

We have a room painted red, one is mauve, another green, a couple are tan. The Hokie Room, popular with Virginia Tech fans (next page), is painted orange and everything in the room is orange, maroon or white, for their school colors.

The goal of decorating at Clay Corner Inn is to combine function with aesthetic appeal. If anything, our rooms are under-decorated. Mister and Lady are not what you'd call trinket people.

Here are a few little decorating tips to keep in mind. Things grouped together look better in odd numbers. People like to put their feet up. Precious antiques can make people nervous. Pictures can be hung next to an easy chair at eye level when seated, or over a table at eye level when seated.

Angled furniture or pieces away from a wall can make a room more interesting. Mirrors make small spaces appear larger. Dried wreaths and arrangements in guest rooms bother some people. Colorful front doors are welcoming. Throw pillows and baskets can go anywhere.

Dogs should have a basket for their toys, even if they only go there to take them out, not ever to put them back.

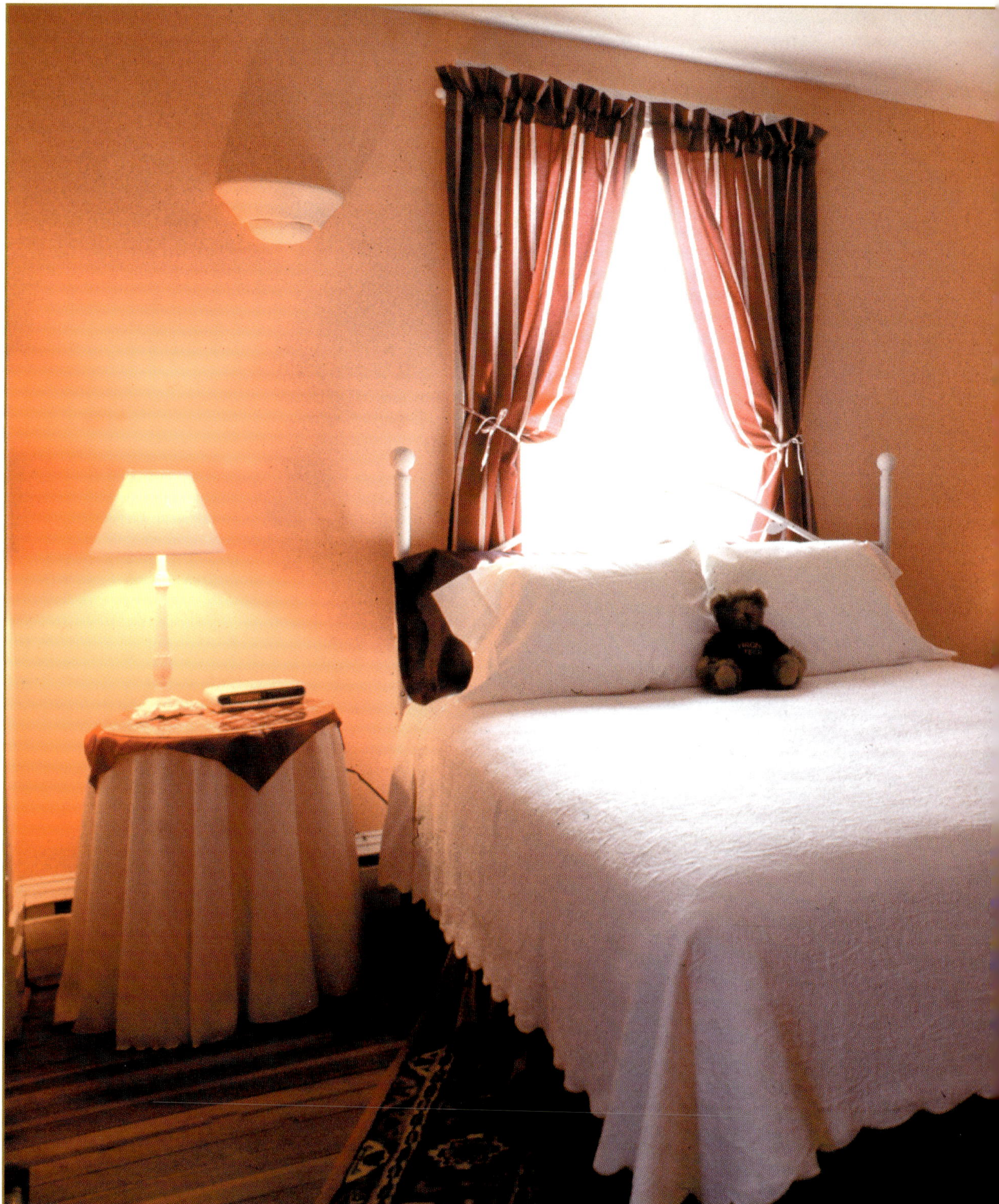

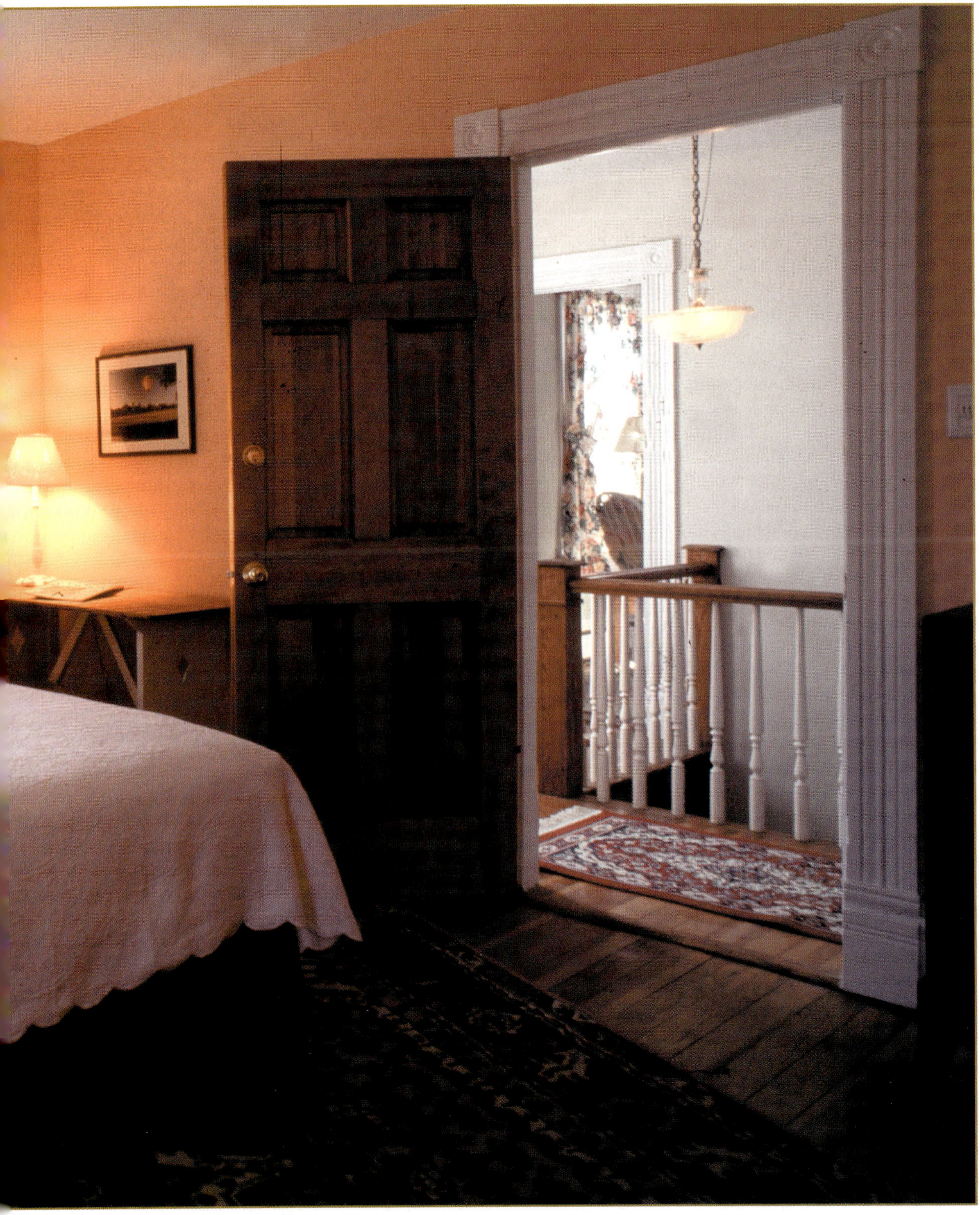

17

The Bathroom

    My bathroom is the great outdoors, although I'm selective about the particular places I use. Of course, Number One is more often a communications exercise than a relief activity, especially on the Huckleberry Trail where I note with my nose which dogs have already been there and let them know that I was there, too.
    "There" is loosely defined as a particular leaf or branch or trunk or post or whatever is holding the messages of the day. It's like e-mail in that it's a communications method. Not like e-mail because it's not electronic. Actually, *c'est tres naturel.*
    Number Two is generally done in the woods or shrubbery where no one will notice. If it's less than two feet from the trail, Mister will collect it and take it away with us, to be disposed of in a proper trash receptacle.
    By contrast, the guest bathrooms here are quite limited and range in size from the smallest, 5 1/2 feet by 6 1/2 feet to the largest, 8 1/2 feet by 13 feet . There are 23 items on the cleaning list and almost as many things on the inspection form. Certainly I could never dream up half as many tasks to tend to in such a small space for the purpose of washing oneself or otherwise engaging in bathroom activities.
    There are more than two dozen items just on the bathroom outfitting list. Rugs, wastebasket, toilet paper holder, towel racks, hook, shower rod and hooks, shower curtain and liner, rubber bath mat inside tub, cloth bath mat over shower rod, deodorant soap in the shower, face soap in the soap dish, liquid soap, shampoo, shower cap, lotion, drinking cups, lights, fan, air freshener, tissues, hair dryer, extra light bulbs, mirror, little piece of furniture, plunger, toilet bowl brush,

towels and facecloths - whew, I'm exhausted just writing about it.

Of course, not only must one have all these things, but also they must be color coordinated. The shower curtain should connect to the color scheme in the guest room. Even if the bath towels are both white, they must be the exact same white ones with the exact same style and border pattern. Same with the hand towels and facecloths.

The bath towels do not have to match the hand towels or face cloths, but each two of the same item must be identical. Do you understand that? And if you do, can you imagine why? Because Lady is picky, that's why. Mister will be the first one to tell you that she comes from a long line of picky people.

I'll get into lots of trouble if I write about them, the in-laws. Suffice it to say that too many of them prefer cats to dogs and that alone draws a mental picture of the tense, albeit mutually tolerant, relationship that exists.

New bathrooms cost somewhere between $5,000 and $10,000. Do you know what kind of a dog house that kind of money can buy? Doghouse *sans toilette*, mind you.

Our bathrooms are not the luxury kind with the eight-dog (two-person) whirlpool tubs and enough space for a little dinner party. Clay Corner Inn baths are functional, and some that were here when we bought the place are very small. When Mister renovated the Huckleberry House, he did a great job of planning bathrooms that are a little larger. He designed four-foot vanities in every one, bathtubs and showers and a strip of very bright lights over a huge mirror, even in the ones with natural light through a window. He's a clever man, Mister is.

Photo by author

18

Amenities

An *amenity*, according to *Random House Webster's Dictionary* is "a feature that provides comfort, convenience or pleasure." Well, the word *feature* is a little overstated. One can say my treats are amenities, but they don't fall into the feature category.

Feature is defined in the same dictionary with significant words like *prominent* and *conspicuous* and *special attraction.* Something like a T-bone steak, one complete coffeecake, pound of bacon – now we're talking feature. I would define *amenity* as a trifle little something that's nice, like a mini-muffin, small dog treat, slice of bacon.

In the lodging business, the first thought when one mentions amenities is those little soaps, shampoo, lotion, etc. My first amenity of this type was at the Washington Dulles Airport Marriott where I spent a night before flying to Denver for a 10-day Colorado vacation. I was 10 1/2 months old and in training as a future Leader Dog, so it was no vacation *pour moi.*

We checked into the hotel the afternoon before our flight, and I immediately headed into the bathroom to investigate. I jumped in the bathtub, behind the curtain and started chewing on the little soap package. Not much else to do in there, no water, no toys.

Mister and Lady took it away from me. "No, no. Don't eat soap," they said. I saw the amenities up next to the sink and was about to jump up – chewable-looking things they were — but my bathroom adventure was terminated, and I had to go to the bedroom. There I found a nice-sized plastic wastebasket to chew. It was promptly taken away and after sniffing every corner and under the bed, I settled down in complete boredom on the floor.

Guest room amenities have increased over recent years, and now, in addition to shower soap, facial soap and shampoo as a minimum, people travelers expect lotion, hair dryers, irons and ironing boards, clock radios, data ports and other niceties. The upscale inns and hotels also provide little sewing kits, mouthwash, shoe polish cloths, bathrobes, chocolates and any number of luxurious frivolities.

Dog travelers are becoming more accepted. More than half of U.S. lodging establishments let us stay with them. They're catering to me and my canine compatriots big-time to get our owners' money.

At certain hotels, pet amenities include "Pawier" water (San Ysidro Ranch, Montecito, CA), pillows, biscuits, pet massage, bowls, special meals from a pet menu and a toy. At the Four Seasons in New York City, the doormen keep dog treats in their pockets. I think I'll go there and spend the afternoon walking in and out of the door. Other hotels have extra leashes and dog food on hand.

Someone might suggest that I'm an amenity here at Clay Corner Inn – a dog to pet and talk to and roll on the floor with. But refrain, OK? I do not wish to be placed in any category that includes shampoo and soap!

19

Housekeeping

Housekeeping is a big part of this business, and readily explains why you'll never find a dog owning an inn. If you even think about getting into this business, you better love everything about cleaning and know all about cleansers, dirt, stains, mildew and dust and the supplies and equipment to deal with these things.

Now there is one item of great interest here - the woolie-on-a-stick. It makes a fine toy - like a two-for-one deal - the woolie and the stick. I shredded a couple of new ones once. Now they're kept in a closet, except when in use. I've been told not to expect another one. However, it's nice to know that if you're not near a pet shop or toy department when you need to buy a gift for a dog, one of these is sure to please.

More time is spent on cleaning around here than most other tasks added together. There are so many things to do in each guest room after a guest leaves that Lady can't fit it all on one page, single-spaced, without reducing the typestyle down to eight or nine points!

The shower is sprayed and wiped down; the drain is checked; the rubber bath mat is picked up and cleaned on the bottom (where no one even sees it!); the shower liner should be checked (this gets overlooked occasionally, I hear); the sink and mirror are cleaned; light bulbs are wiped; trash removed and new liner put in the little wastebasket; toilets get cleaned and flushed; everything is dusted; the floor is wiped spotless.

And then the rugs are shaken and placed back on the floor parallel to the edges of the bathroom.

And if that's not picky enough, if someone walks back into the bathroom for some reason - like they forgot to corner the toilet paper or check for an extra roll - she must walk around these rugs. If you get a footprint on a bathroom rug, it must be shaken and put down again - still parallel to the nearest edge.

In the bedroom, they change the bed and continue this dusting, cleaning, straightening, mopping, vacuuming routine until the room looks like no one was ever in it before. I guess that's the idea, but check out some of the pickiest little things. Seams, for example.

All the pillowcases, and there are four pillows on every big bed, must be ironed completely smooth and then positioned with the seam side down. Now, I am certain that I speak for the entire canine world and a significant portion of the human world when I say "Does anyone really care what way the seam on the pillowcase is facing? Could this minor detail change your mind about where you're lodging for the night or disrupt your efforts to sleep?"

All the lampshade seams must face the back so no one can see them. And the seams on the curtain tiebacks should face down.

To facilitate all this hoopla about cleaning, there are cleansers and cleaning supplies everywhere. Time is money, and going in search of a paper towel or some window cleaner reduces efficiency. Personally, I'm amazed they don't park a couple vacuum cleaners in every room.

Photo by author

And this is just the guest rooms. All the common areas, front entrance, kitchens, stairs and railings, hallways, rugs and outdoor furniture must constantly be wiped and cleaned. We power-wash the outside of the buildings once or twice a year.

Even cats don't require such fastidious housekeeping. We rescued a 3-week-old wild kitten from a wood pile next door one Fall. She was tame enough to handle and sniff within 48 hours, and in her second 48 hours at Clay Corner Inn, she moved into my crate! Speck of a thing with respect to my five-foot by three-foot office, but she never complained about the fur, dirt or arrangement of my bedding and toys.

She just found a place about the size of a tea cup and curled up. She wasn't much trouble so I let her stay for a month.

20

Laundry

I've been attracted to laundry since I was a puppy. Dirty socks especially, but everything else runs a close second. Socks have many advantages. They stretch nicely. They can be carried all in a ball or just barely by a single tooth, and the whole sock follows. They have more intense smells than say a pillowcase or sweatshirt, and they're much easier to fling in the air and play with.

The laundry habit of me and most of my friends seems to annoy adults. This is perplexing, to say the least, when they should be flattered and pleased. Why? Because the main reason we like laundry is because we LOVE our people. Dirty laundry has their body odor on it, and it's an extension of their presence that we can have near and dear to us in their absence.

Absence, of course, can be loosely defined as "across the room" or "in the next room" or "on another continent." Basically, if they're not petting us, playing with us or preparing our food, our people are absent, and raiding laundry is a desirable means of having part of them with us.

Well, in the B&B business, laundry accumulates very quickly. We have four washers and dryers of various vintage here at Clay Corner Inn, and they are in motion the better part of eight hours a day. If you have any aversion whatsoever to washing machines, dryers or folding sheets and towels endlessly, better reconsider getting into this line of work.

When Mister first looked into commercial laundry equipment in 1997, Lady said she didn't think it was necessary. Then she changed her tune, and guess what Mister said? Actually, I didn't hang around for that conversation. The bottom line, as near as I have determined, is that we can't get any commercial equipment into the main house basement, even if we take off doors and trim.

Commercial equipment is large - in size and price, but energy efficiency and staff productivity are also considerations. In our case, being a multiple building property, it makes sense to have laundry equipment in each house, rather than moving all the laundry between buildings. So some things have a way of working out for the best.

Seems like a big waste of water and time to me, but humans are meticulous, compared to dogs, about these things. And Lady is particular about the whole process - setting and starting the washing machine, putting in the soap, waiting for it to dissolve before putting in sheets; washing sheets and towels separately, pairs of pillowcases together, lights and darks and reds in different loads, bleach with white only, stain remover on spots, cold water for dark things, so many details, boggles my brain.

The laundry area is organized with a laundry basket and plastic shoebox container for every house. Sheets, towels and supplies go in the baskets for the houses. Pillowcases go in the plastic containers to be ironed. After they are ironed, they're placed in the laundry basket for the particular house. Each morning, whoever goes to a guest house first, takes the basket and puts away the laundry and supplies.

My major interest in the laundry process is getting my stuffed toys back when Lady takes them for a wash and dirtying them up as soon as possible.

65

21

Reservations

I have some reservations about certain things – roller coasters, for example, and cats in the house. Actually, cats in the house might be fun, but it would raise havoc with Lady's order. When I get involved in a chase, I become totally absorbed in the object of the chase – lamps, rugs, people, furniture notwithstanding.

Oops, wrong word meaning. This is supposed to be about guest reservations. Some guests probably have reservations, too. Especially those who have never stayed at a B&B. When a guest has reservations about making a reservation, we assure them that they'll have the amenities of a hotel, comforts of a home and friendliness of a small inn.

Then we tell them that we have a blank-blank-blank (1-2-3) something rating with a major national association, which I can't name here. To use their logo and name in writing, one needs to participate in their special advertising program, and that's not in our budget. But saying it verbally is legal and usually allays reservations about making reservations. Oops, wrong word meaning, again.

Most of our reservations are made via telephone, although a greater percentage each year is accepted by e-mail. In the beginning, we kept information in a notebook, two pages per day. Then Vanessa Oetjens came to work for us. What an organizer.

After she put order into laundry, linens, ironing, closets and other places, she turned to Mister and Lady: "I know you love your notebook, but I know a much better reservation system, and I can set it up, and it's easy."

Lady likes easy, so she approved it. And we're still using it. It's a simple chart

Amy Crawford

of small boxes with dates across the top and room numbers down the side. Tape goes on the board to cover booked dates for each room. Information is written on a reservation card that's filed by date.

Some small inns have computerized reservations systems, and some allow guests to make reservations on-line through a reservation site on the Web. We don't do that. For one, we don't have one computer that can be dedicated to reservations. When that phone rings, we need to be able to give a prompt, accurate response. We also shut the computer off during thunder and lightning storms, but the phones keep working – and ringing.

Also, someone may be booking our last room online at the same time we're booking it by telephone. Overbooking is a situation one does not like to find oneself in. Now if you overbooked with dogs, not one dog would fuss about having to share a room or having to sleep on the living room couch. Not so with people. We must be very careful to keep them in separate rooms.

While we prefer having reservations in advance so we can forecast labor and breakfast volume, we do accept some walk-ins, and we're always prepared for extra breakfast guests.

On the flip side, it's very kind for guests to let us know if they will not be coming for breakfast. Of course, I am right there to eat their portions, but I don't get them. Mister and Lady have reservations about feeding me too much.

22

Business Travelers

These guests are a vital part of our business, and they're loved by innkeepers everywhere for their mid-week, often multiple night reservations and repeat stays. Some of them don't have as much time to spend with me as the weekend people, and admittedly, my blond fur doesn't go well on some of those dark suits.

Fortunately for me, we have people like Tom McAdoo, Rich Swope and Kevin Stacey of Mike's Video in State College, PA. Oh, I should mention Mike Negra, the owner, who comes sometimes, and his wife, Wanda White. She brought her parents to see me on their way to Florida.

They come to visit their downtown store, Mike's Movies & Music, and they don't wear suits. They are what one might call super ultra casual – the music industry is that way, I think. Have you seen how some of the rock stars are dressed?

Well, these music people L-O-V-E me. They like the breakfast and atmosphere and pool, too, but they see me way before they see breakfast, atmosphere or pool.

Lori Wagner of Honeywell comes often, too, and she brings me things. And she kisses me! Kevin O'Boyle and Susan LeFave from Sun Microsystems were here when I had a little ear infection and a skin rash. Susan checked on me every day. She knows a lot about dogs, and has a brown Labrador named Jasper who's the same age as I am. I hope he comes with her next time.

Clark Tibbetts comes almost every week, and he brought his wife, Kathleen, and their dog, Sage, once. Sage is a Tennessee hound, and they didn't let him get on the bed.

Rob Warner with VTLS, Inc. in Blacksburg has been our guest many times over six years. He telecommutes from his home in Tennessee, and we're great pals.

Business travelers are very considerate, low maintenance and gone most all day. They also are willing to pay a fair rate for a nice place. Anyone who has traveled in cities, and I have, knows it's hard to find a nice room for less than $200. When this book was printed, our mid-week rates were still under $100, including a fabulous breakfast and my presence.

Photo by author

I give them a very warm welcome and the time and space to play with me. This is good for them. Petting dogs is a proven stress reducer, and traveling away from home on business can be a stressful event.

Our business travelers are generous with their time and knowledge. John Spencer of Microsoft offers assistance when he comes from Redmond, Wash. Mary Kay Cunningham of Vatex, Inc. in Richmond supplies us with catalogs and ideas for promotional items.

Jim Allred of Engineering Vision and Innovation, Inc. in Columbia, Md., has straightened out a few things on our computer. Allred went to Virginia Tech, and his parents, J.B. and Cherie Allred of Skaneateles, NY, are good friends of Mister and Lady. I've been to their house.

They have a 14-pound, yellow tabby cat named Bear. We stared at each other, excitement brimming inside me, disgust and annoyance all over Bear's face. He wouldn't run, so there was no chase. They need a dog to mellow out this cat-with-an-attitude.

Since we serve breakfast between 7:30 and 9 on weekday mornings, our business travelers are able to get to 8 a.m. meetings wide-awake and comfortably full. No excuse for them not being bright-eyed and bushy-tailed. (Love that expression; love those squirrels!)

To innkeepers who say that business travelers come from out of town, so it's hard to get them, we say, "all those business travelers come to see someone in town, so call on all the places in town where someone might visit." We have business travelers who go to the local Ford dealer (both my mobile crates are Fords), bookstores, manufacturing plants, engineering firms, radio stations, gift shops, churches, restaurants, the hospital, banks and lots of other places. Maybe even the local pet store.

What a brilliant idea ! I need to get brochures to the pet store! Where's Mister? Where's Lady? Where are the car keys for the mobile crate? Let's go to the pet store! Right now! Woof!

23

Special Events

I'd like to see a dog show or dog party for a special event, but it hasn't happened yet. We have had a few small meetings, reunions and weddings, but the guests didn't bring any dogs. I need to work on our policy of not accepting dogs, except dog guides. They can go anywhere, of course.

Special events are most often thought of in terms of additional revenue. Our experience indicates that the revenue is balanced pretty evenly with labor and expenses. So we usually do events only when there are overnight rooms involved. We are primarily in the lodging business.

If we had more dog events, we wouldn't need so much labor to prepare food that looks pretty on dishes that need to be washed later. One could really just knock the food from the counter to the floor. Steak would be the entrée, complemented with some other meat and apples. I like apples, and Lady sometimes lets me eat apple pieces.

But for people events, like everything else I've written about, there are many considerations to make them happy. For meetings, participants need certain chair and table arrangements, good lighting, excellent food and beverage service and temperature control. We also provide ice water, little candies, and notepads and pens. Coffee breaks and audio-visual equipment can be arranged.

Family reunions and weddings are lots of fun for me. Everyone is happy, and there's a greater chance that I can get some appetizer or something. Notice how happy people and good food go together? In fact, here's an observation in favor of people.

I've never seen a person bite or snarl at another person when one reached for a barbecued chicken wing or corn chip. Dogs squabble over food share much more than people do. Maybe it would be a good idea to have separate bowls for a dog event.

We had a small wedding once in January, 32 in attendance plus the bride and groom. We've done a wedding brunch, bridal shower, rehearsal dinner – all on a small scale. Most of the time, I'm allowed to wander around the parties.

A few luncheons and wine and cheese parties have also been held at Clay Corner Inn. Luncheon is just lunch. The –eon on the end indicates it's a fancy lunch. I never get lunch – unless I'm able to scrounge some *pieces de la luncheon*.

The wine and cheese parties have been held in December so everything was decorated with candles and Christmas garland and lights. It was real pretty. I stayed in the main house and refrained from both wine and cheese.

I was supposed to wear a red ribbon, but that didn't last long. I'm happy in my natural coat and a collar. Sometimes I'll wear a bandanna for a special occasion and so will Kent, but that's all. No hats, sweaters, booties or bows. I've worn a sock a few times when I had a cut on my leg. The minute Mister or Lady look the other way, I take it off. Socks make good toys, but I'm not interested in wearing them.

Perhaps I can coordinate some event like the Yappy Hours held in Jefferson, LA. They're parking lot parties with food and drink for all. The $10 donation goes to the Jefferson SPCA. Sounds like a good idea for a special event.

Kent

24

Negotiation

My negotiating skills have improved over time, and usually involve my having something firmly clenched between my teeth. Basket of muffins, teddy bear, sneaker – something along those lines.

Mister will wrench things away from me, but other times, I release my grip on the promise of a treat. And they're good to follow through, and I get a treat. Doesn't seem like I should get a treat for taking something I shouldn't have, but hey, it works for me. That's successful negotiation.

The first time someone walked into Clay Corner Inn and made a cash offer for a three-night stay at a reduced rate during a slow time, Lady was taken aback. Thinking fast on her feet, she said "doesn't include breakfast," and a deal was struck.

Price negotiation always begs the question: When is a fast nickel worth more than a slow dime? There are innkeepers who don't budge off their rates, others who take anything to get the business, and the rest who fall somewhere in between.

People love to believe they're getting a deal, and there are other things besides price that are negotiable. Payment terms like cash in advance; accommodations such as upgraded room or extra amenities; no breakfast as cited in the example above; limited maid service for a long-term stay; restricted use of recreational equipment; and so on.

The only non-negotiable thing I know of is giving attention to the innkeeper dog. This must never be limited or reduced. This innkeeper dog is available for attention and entertainment all the time to all the guests.

My friend Trout

    Rates and negotiation define a bed and breakfast the same way price evokes any image. While one certainly doesn't want to become known as a bargain basement in lodging, income is real money, and it makes sense to be a little flexible during slow times or early years in business.
    One can dicker for a multi-million dollar yacht, a yard sale lawn mower, most pieces of real estate and even – as hard as it is to write – even for the price of a dog. Innkeepers and other business people should not think a potential customer is cheap or doesn't think a product or service is worth the asking price just because he or she tries to strike deal.
    Herein lies one of the benefits of being self-employed: You can make the rules and decide whether or not to play the game, without apology.

25

Checking In

Although we officially post 3 - 9 p.m. as check-in time, we let guests check in whenever they want before 3 p.m. if their room is ready. If it's not ready, I suggest they play with me until it is. They can also use the restroom, leave luggage, park their car and walk to Virginia Tech or downtown.

Some guests, especially those coming from overseas, arrive on late flights into Washington, D.C., or Roanoke, VA, and come to Clay Corner Inn very late or the next morning.

Well, I'm on duty for this job most of the time. With four feet instead of two, and not generally being distracted at the computer or in the middle of something more pressing than a nap, it's easy for me to be at the door first. I grab a toy or magazine on the way, start to wiggle and wag my tail and look positively thrilled to see whoever walks through the door. Which I am.

And I'm teaching Kent, our junior innkeeper dog-in-training, all about check-in duties. The first couple of times that Kent heard the doorbell, he barked. I rolled my eyes. The next few times, he ran around the dining room because that's where the doorbell sound is heard.

He is a smart dog and before the end of his first week, Kent learned to associate the sound in the dining room with a person at the door. He realized that these people come in peace, so there's no need to bark at them. After that, he just began to follow my lead.

Of course, I want a good sniff right away - you know where, but I've modified my greeting to be more socially acceptable to humans. Dogs are different in this way, and we dogs agree that our manner of checking each other out is not only acceptable, but imperative to establish a host of details on which I will not elaborate here.

So let's say here come two guests. Dog-loving guests. They ring the bell and walk in the door. They see us, they gush, they ohh and ahh, they begin to pet us. I love them instantly. They are amused; we are amused. I hope they are staying for several weeks.

On the flip side, let's say here come two guests who are not crazy about dogs. (What's their problem, I want to know.) They move right past us while I get as good a sniff as possible (often I smell cat which explains the problem) and then I return their attitude. I take my toy or magazine and plop down on the rug where they'll have to walk over or around me, and I pretend I don't notice them. The next dog-loving guest will more than make up for their ambivalence.

About this time, some human innkeeper appears, and the welcome program begins. Registration cards are completed and the plethora of information flows. Breakfast time and location, where to park, the pool, the hot tub, the ice machine, the soda, etc.

Everything we tell them at check-in is posted or can be found in the notebook in each guest room. The notebooks serve many purposes, the main one being that Mister and Lady do not have to continually repeat the story of how old the houses are, why the twin houses were built; how long we've been in business; and how much we like it. The latter is directly related to repair and maintenance events over, say, the past 48 hours.

The check-in procedure is real important. It's the second or third impression of the property - the first being telephone or e-mail correspondence and the second, the curb appeal of actually seeing the property. But it's the first live interaction, and it must be warm and friendly, while maintaining a professional demeanor.

For example, we don't hug our guests. If a repeat guest gestures to hug one of us, we oblige. It's nice, but it's not our place to initiate the action.

I exercise discretion in matters like how friendly I should be. One needs to evaluate a guest's mood and personality fairly quickly to make important decisions like whether or not to roll over and propose that they scratch my belly.

Likewise, the innkeepers are sensitive to whether or not a guest wants to be chatty or just get to the room and be left alone. When Mister and Lady travel, they fall into the second category, so they're sensitive to others who just want the basic information and some privacy. Me, social animal that I am, I fall in the first category. Chat, chat, chat all you want, just keep that belly rubbed and I'll keep that hind leg moving!

My friend Trout (on right)

26

Checking Out

Lady and I handle most of the check-outs. I let her do the paperwork and money part. I stick with the PR stuff. She prepares the check-out slips, along with special receipts for government travelers the night before. You see, there is as much work in the evenings as in the mornings, not to mention all afternoon.

Government guests need to take a receipt that breaks out the breakfast expense and the tax from the lodging per diem rate. We treat the B&B rate like an airline ticket, and breakfast is part of the deal. You can't separate your airline meal from the actual trip on the airplane.

On the other hand, at Clay Corner Inn, we do a lot of business with government people, so we see that they have what they need to prove they bought lodging and breakfast here, instead of a puppy or a piece of furniture or something.

Speaking of puppies, Mister and Lady tell people we take cash, checks, traveler's checks, MasterCard, VISA, American Express, diamonds, laptop computers and hard labor for payment. I think we should take puppies, too. But don't bring one (or two). She said that she will not change her mind even if I write that in this book.

Most people pay with a credit card, and we are very happy the bank persuaded us to buy electronic equipment the first year. Besides looking professional, it's very easy.

And speaking of looking professional, the charge for processing credit cards should be considered one of the costs of being in business. It doesn't look very professional to offer a discount for cash or check. Along the same vein, local phone calls here really cost 10 cents each, but we say it's free and include it in the room rate.

Our staff can go over check-out details and accept payment, but most guests like to connect with Mister or Lady Innkeeper before departing - to thank them, tell how wonderful things were for them (or any constructive suggestions they may have), and to say how neat it was to see me and Kent.

All the compliments are treasured. It truly is hard work every day, and when someone appreciates it as much as many of our guests, it makes the rest of the day's work just a little lighter.

Late check-outs are honored when possible, often Sunday mornings when guests return from church after the noon check-out time. Many people vacate the room and just need to leave their car parked at our place for the day.

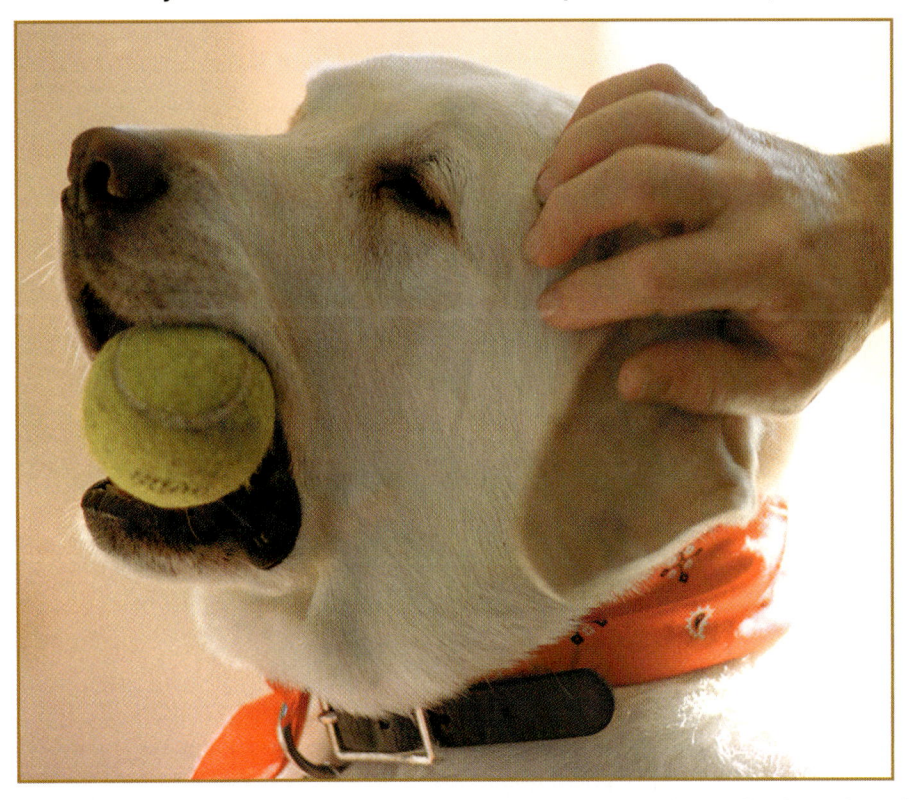

And there are the early departs - guests with early flights or those who just want to get on the road for a long drive. We offer to put breakfast in their guest house kitchen, with homemade cereal, banana and muffin. We'll put milk and juice in the refrigerator, load the coffee pot and set the table. This is appreciated greatly by many, and Lady doesn't think anyone should start their day without a little nourishment. I agree with that. Of course, I don't get to see them before leaving and that's a disappointment for both of us, I suspect.

Many of our guests make future reservations at check-out time, get on waiting lists and buy a T-shirt or a book. Lots of them just like to chat before leaving. Psychologically, I think it gives closure to their stay.

Just imagine driving down the highway after a weekend at Clay Corner Inn and suddenly realizing you don't have closure. Now what? Oh, my, keep your eyes on the road!

Drive back for closure or continue on your way feeling open-ended? Tough decision. Oh, my. I say go back and pet the innkeeper dogs a final time for proper closure.

27

Employees

As a full-time innkeeper dog, I work for room and board and recognition, which would cost quite a bit considering the lifestyle to which I have become accustomed. I have my own office crate 30 inches wide, 4 feet long and almost 3 feet high. This doubles as a table for the television, camera, iron and miscellaneous things in the main inn office and is furnished with a comforter, a pillow or two, assorted toys and tennis balls. I re-arrange this on a regular basis to suit my mood, and sometimes I put some paper, a pen, a sneaker or a catalog in it.

Kent has a crate right next to mine, but he doesn't like it. We think he was raised in a kennel. I can see that he's afraid that he'll be locked in the crate, but Mister and Lady never close the crate doors. He'll learn. He's smart.

Our portable crate (a.k.a. Ford Explorer) doubles as a means of transportation for daily errands as well as extended vacations. I like having a pool in the yard and a walking trail on the next block. I have three collars in different styles, some doggie packs for serious hiking, a couple of leashes and my own dishes. I'm compensated fairly.

As I understand the human side of employment, people work for basically the same things, but they get money to buy their room and board elsewhere, and they appreciate recognition, too.

Since cleaning is such a big part of this business, it's imperative to find people who like to clean, or at the least, will take the job seriously enough to ensure that all the details that Lady is so picky about get done to her standards. And the AAA standards. And the health department standards.

And, above all, guess who? The guest's standards. As Lady says many times,

Solomon & Kent

"the guest writes our paychecks - I only sign them." This is a guest-driven enterprise.

One thing to keep in mind about job descriptions and associated pay rates, beyond that all applicants be crazy about dogs - or at least innkeeper dogs - is that one will spend about the same amount of money for labor whether or not you pay minimum wage. The difference is where the money goes.

When one pays minimum wage, lots of money is spent in turnover, advertising, training, stress and one's own back-breaking labor between employees. The other option is putting the money in the employees' paycheck. Along with recognition in the newsletter and in person, positive feedback, encouragement, and Clay Corner Inn T-shirts, polo shirts or sweatshirts, our employees receive an above average hourly rate.

For a real break, however, every innkeeper should train someone to prepare and serve breakfast, handle reservations and office details, and check people in and out. This provides necessary breaks when the innkeeper(s) can go out for lunch, pet the dogs, walk to a cafe, walk the dogs, visit a friend, read a book, relax and play exclusively with the innkeeper dogs.

Lady has given a few talks at innkeeper conferences and one was about hiring and keeping employees. She made a list of 32 ways to make people feel good. I can think of 32 ways to make a dog feel good, too, but no one invites me to conferences.

Who knows? Just maybe when this book is published, I can go to an innkeeping conference and present a few tips on innkeeper dogs and stuff.

28

Money

The canine world measures riches in terms of companionship, along with simple things like food and water, a good cat or rabbit chase and doghouses and pillows. As pack animals, dogs are highly social, and a rich life is one that is shared with others - dogs or people, maybe a cat or two or an extraordinary barnyard animal.

Money is a very important part of the human world, and we try to collect as much as we can. I prefer checks and cash over credit cards because we must go to the bank to deposit them, and I get dog treats at the bank. That's my simple outlook on money.

But before we even get money, we have to establish rates. And in the lodging business, there's always the consideration of rate vs. occupancy. One can charge a lower than average rate and generate a high occupancy. With a higher rate and less business, one can actually get the same revenue. Also, rates reflect image.

Of course, a general rule of thumb (or paw pad in my case) is to look around at what others are doing. Before writing this book, for example, we looked at lots of other dog books. I really liked O. Henry's very short story *Memoirs of a Yellow Dog,* published in 1906.

Lady does an annual check of rates being charged by the other lodging establishments in our area. Then we analyze the benefits of staying at our place, the added value of an innkeeper dog or two, and we set a price. Take it or leave it. Or negotiate. See Negotiation chapter.

In our business, we accept many reservations for the government per diem rate because of our location next to Virginia Tech. All state and federal employees are subject to a ridiculously low rate that has not changed in more than six years. Lady wrote a letter to the big people in Richmond about this, but she never got an answer. She told them about how her expenses had gone up in six and a half years, especially for food, labor, utilities and supplies.

    She didn't mention dog food, but inflation hasn't escaped the big names in the multi-billion dollar dog food business either. Do you know what they do?? The price remains the same, while the size of the bag goes down. What used to be a 20-pound sack of dry dog food is now 17.5 pounds. Think we're stupid? Not Lady. She notices these things. She has observations, too. She's just not making a book out of them.

    Beyond the dog treats, I don't get involved in money matters. I observe some wrangling about things like new roofs. We've had four new roofs in three years - one on every house in the B&B complex. Any idea what those cost? Try $30,000, roughly. One year we put in underground utilities to the tune of around $5,000. No one notices this either, but it definitely enhances the property.

    Budgeting, projecting, saving money and spending money are pretty much common sense issues. I think it goes like this: you spend less than you collect during the strong months, save the difference and spend it during the slow months. If one is lucky, there's a little bit left over, and you can spend it on a vacation with the dog. If there's not enough for a vacation, a small dog toy or one of those woolie things on a stick will be fine.

Lady is cautious about spending money on major additions and improvements that don't generate revenue. But she doesn't want raindrops on guests' heads either, thus the new roofs. Mister and Lady manage the money well enough, but there are always surprises. In the last year alone, surprise buys included two new washing machines, one dryer, a swimming pool liner, two rooms of new furniture, gas-powered hedge trimmers and a new gas fireplace.

And a dog bed from Orvis. That was an impulse buy. I got on it in the Orvis store so they bought it for me. Next time we go shopping, I think I'll climb into a new Lincoln Navigator and see what happens.

85

29

Maintenance

I'm here to tell you that maintenance is right up there with breakfast for a daily event - for all of us. And it is mandatory that innkeepers and innkeeper dogs be handy, creative and knowledgeable about almost everything inside and outside of a house.

My duties are numerous with "Territorial Inspection Notwithstanding Kitty and Litter Evacuation" (TINKLE) topping the list for my most time-consuming maintenance-related activity. I also keep the grounds squirrel-free. During the summer, I check the swimming pool water many times each day, removing tennis balls and floating toys that occasionally sail into it. Mister monitors the chemical aspect of the water and keeps the heater and filter systems at both the pool and the hot tub in good working order.

It only took one trip into the hot tub for me to conclude that this is one body of water I don't like. Too hot. It's kept at 104 degrees, whereas the pool is only around 86. I jumped in one spring day when Mister opened the pool, and it was 46 degrees. I liked it just fine.

I intentionally don't get involved in some maintenance projects. Take painting, for example. Luggage, chairs and assorted objects collide with walls and doorways all the time in this business. When I show up, all I hear is "Don't step here, don't lean there, don't let you tail brush this wall, you may not chew or tug on the drop cloth, and please don't walk under the ladder." The last thing has nothing to do with superstition and everything to do with my size and lack of acute attention to where I am walking.

If I move a hammer, shake a rag, play with tools or rearrange and tidy up newspapers, I might be scolded. The whole newspaper scene is a source of great confusion. Sometimes they want the sections separated. Other times they all go together in a neat pile for recycling. Then I come around a corner one day and find newspapers unfolded and spread out all over the floor. I've heard that some people train their dogs to pee on newspapers. I'd get into trouble if I did that.

Quiet yard work is more to my liking. Clearing brush, weeding flowers, pruning bushes, chewing sticks and moving mulch are jobs where I can contribute. The keyword here is quiet. When the lawn mower, weed eater, hedge clippers, chain saw or other gas- or electric-powered piece of equipment comes out, I go in.

Among the myriad maintenance tasks are planting flowers, pulling weeds, washing windows, cleaning gutters, sealing the driveway, caring for houseplants, sorting recyclables and hauling trash, unclogging toilets, tightening and refinishing furniture, changing filters, checking smoke alarms, turning mattresses, replacing nuts, bolts and washers, laundering drapes - the list is endless, as well as repetitive.

Second to the chain saw for raucous noise is the snowblower. Mister is very conscientious about snow

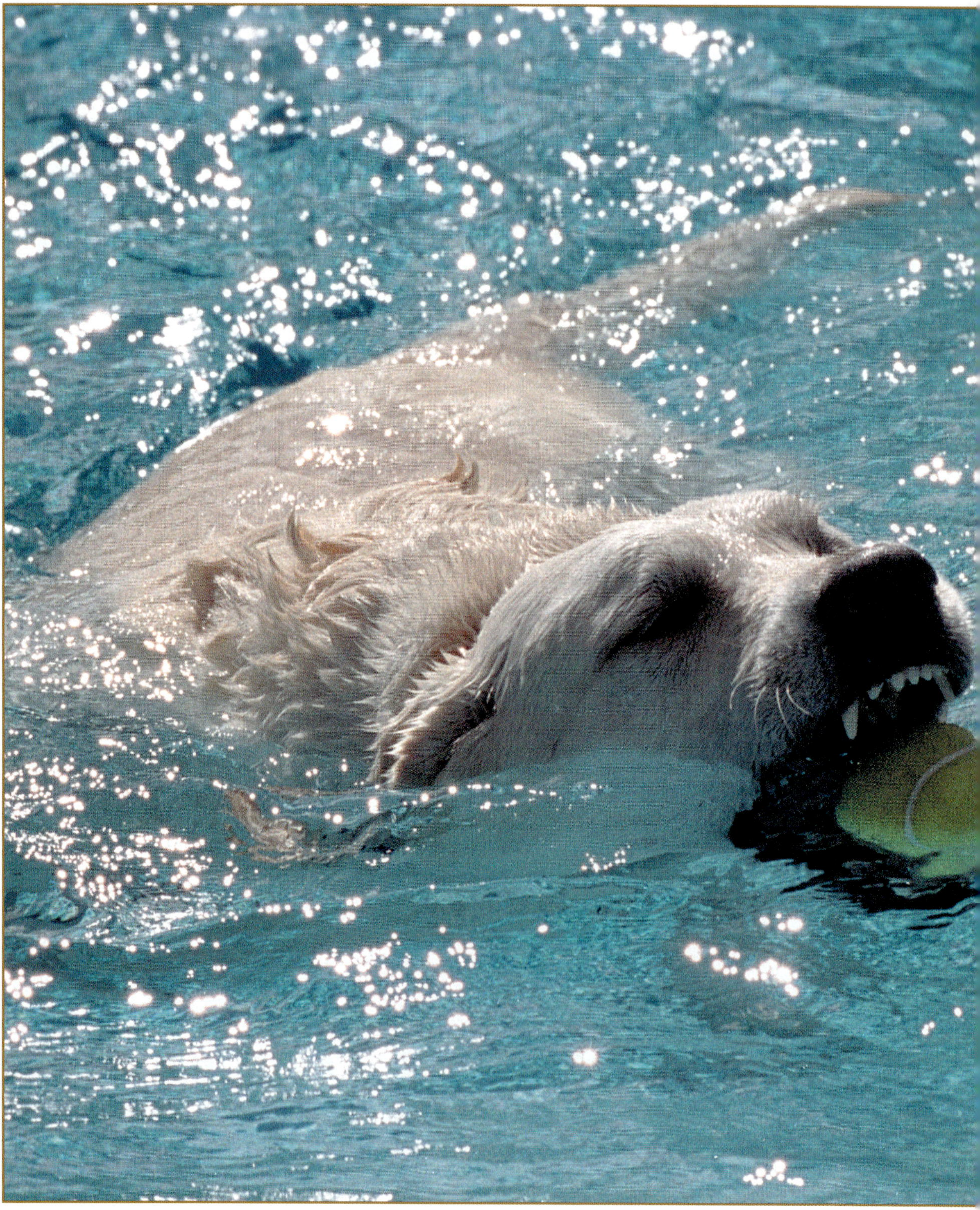

removal. He clears our main driveway and some 400 feet of sidewalk in front of the four B&B houses. Next he blows snow off the brick parking areas. Then it's out back clearing the walkways between the houses and then doing a couple of the neighbors' driveways.

We keep a large plastic container of salt outside the kitchen door for very wet or icy mornings. Wood decks can be slippery when wet as well as icy. Fortunately for us, it was Lady who discovered this (not a guest), and rubber mats were placed on the potentially slippery sections. Double fortunate for us, she was not injured.

Many summer nights when the day is coming to a close (without further incident, hopefully) we go out to shut off the pool lights, and I make a final territorial check of the grounds. And there - on the damp sidewalk between the main house and the pool - are the slugs, 2-3 inches long, spotted and slimy - barely moving. Not something dog or person wants to tread upon.

If you have heard that they like beer, you've heard correctly. However, our experience is that you'll run out of beer long before you run out of slugs. No amount of barking affects them, and they definitely do not fall into the category of a "chasable" - these things barely move. I think they are the least interesting living thing with which I've had contact.

Mister de-slugs the sidewalk, and we can go to bed.

30

Repair & Renovation

When I hear the words *broken, fix, renovate, doesn't work* or *needs repair*, I think of something else to do right away. I have seen repair and renovation work, and I want no part of it. It's time-consuming, expensive and frustrating. Besides there's not much I can contribute with my paws. They're not made for using basic hand tools, and I don't like the sound of power tools, battery or electric.

From the 10-cent washer to the $10,000 roof, we've experienced repair work at all levels. In fact, it is repair that Mister and Lady concede is the most stressful and expensive aspect of this business.

Fortunately for us, Mister is a full-time, on-site, highly-skilled, multi-talented, well-educated and experienced *factotum*. That's the title on his business card. It is a very important position, and I don't see how an inn gets along without one.

Not familiar with the word? Mister's sister-in-law, Debbie Cate, was the first one to use it for him. She learned it a long time ago from a spelling list for kids. She's a teacher, and I think she's very smart.

Factotum comes from Latin *facere* meaning "to do" and *totum* meaning "the whole." And that's a superb description of Mister. He can do everything. He grew up on a Wisconsin farm where everything that broke needed to be fixed with whatever tools and supplies were on hand.

All one needs for repair work anyway is a little time, energy, knowledge and money. Or a lot of each. And one must always be prepared for the possibility that a task, however small, may be fraught with pitfalls and perils.

Of course, the classic adage in all repair and renovation work is: If you don't have time to do it right the first time, when will you have time to do it over?

Mister believes every word of this and does things right the first time.

Unfortunately for him, he's more often fixing something someone else did not do correctly the first time, or even the second time. This creates great stress inside him which can be released only with words I dare not print here. If you've repaired anything in your house, you might be familiar with these words.

We renovated the Huckleberry House in 1997-98. A contractor built a new addition, re-arranged the roofline and put on a new roof. Mister and two part-time helpers spent 18 months tearing out walls and ceilings, putting in new wiring, heating system, plumbing stuff, molding, doors and new ceilings. He moved light fixtures and put air conditioning ductwork in the attic. We subcontracted for the replacement windows. The place was a mess. Of course, I enjoyed being over there for that very reason.

Repair work is constant and ranges from broken appliances and equipment to plumbing problems, cracked glass and broken screens, leaky toilets, loose door hinges, door locks that don't line up properly, drywall cracks, wobbly furniture, faulty wiring, pumps and heaters that stop working and a host of other things.

Kent

But there's a silver lining to repair work. Innkeepers end up owning one, or two, or three, or more, of almost every tool known to modern man, along with a plethora of nails, screws, nuts and bolts, wood filler, caulking tubes and caulking guns, wire, picture hanging kits, sandpaper, *ad infinitum*.

The bottom line? Every inn must have a factotum AND an innkeeper dog – for moral support - to assure that things operate well and function properly.

31

Safety

Safety is a big deal with humans, clumsy as they can be. You've probably never seen a dog trip over the edge of a rug that's lying flat on a flat floor. We don't walk into sliding glass doors often either. Since we never file lawsuits, one would think we'd be welcome everywhere.

A muscular build, strong bones and four vertical legs give us Labradors superior stability, and our paw pads are wonderfully made for good traction. But *homo sapiens* need lots of help in this way, which explains the rubber mats in the bathtubs, no-skid strips on the deck, pads under the rugs and handrails on the stairways. All to keep our guests upright.

My eyesight may not be 20-20, but I can still can see where I'm going most of the time, especially at dusk and after dark, when the *homo sapiens* once again need major assistance.

Porch lights, sensor lights, sidewalk lights, landscape lights, a pool light and lamp posts can be found all over the Clay Corner Inn property. Some come on by timers, others by movement, and the rest need to be switched on by manpower every evening. All so the people can find their way safely.

Mister hangs pictures high in hallways so they're not knocked down by shoulders or luggage brushing against them. Imagine the commotion of suitcases, picture frames and guests all tumbling down the stairs. Not a pleasant thought.

One big safety issue around here that you wouldn't find in a dog-operated inn is food sanitation. I don't mind eating old chicken wings or hamburgers and fries I find on the ground. These are especially plentiful after football games. But not

One bacterial cell can multiply into 16 million in 8 hours.

Time	Number of Bacteria
0 min.	1
20 min.	2
40 min.	4
1 hour	8
2 hours	64
3 hours	512
4 hours	4,096
5 hours	32,768
6 hours	262,144
7 hours	2,097,152
8 hours	16,777,216

so with people.

The food sanitation motto at Clay Corner Inn is simple: hot foods hot, cold foods cold, everything clean. Meat is generally the hot concern, milk is the highest cold priority and as I've stated elsewhere in this book, everything is absurdly clean. They sanitize the counters and dishcloths, keep thermometers in the refrigerators and freezers and wash dishes all the time.

They wash their hands all the time, too, including after petting me. They even throw the dishtowels in the laundry after I've dropped them on the floor somewhere. I say shake it out and use it again. I say picky, picky.

However, it is a fact that one bacterial cell can multiply into 16 million in just eight hours. They can double approximately every 20 minutes.

One of the easiest things to do to promote safety is to keep everything in proper working order, check and replace light bulbs as necessary, have fire extinguishers on every floor and smoke alarms in every room and be alert as weather conditions and temperatures change. Mister likes things in proper working order.

Door locks and window locks are installed for guest room security, but door flaps and simple door drapes are fine for me and my four-footed friends.

Most safety and security details are common sense, and we hope our guests bring some [common sense] along with them, too.

32

Advertising

First step to successful advertising: get a dog. Any good-size dog. Then put said dog in your ads. Hint: Don't dress them up, even though William Wegman's gray Weimaraners wear everything from neckties to ball gowns, and they're very famous.

One of my favorite ads on television is for Dirt Devil vacuum cleaners. There are yellow Labrador puppies spilling plants and things to show how wonderfully the product works.

According to an article in *Pet Product News* (July 1999, author Sheila Sobell), ad agencies promote using dogs because of physical characteristics. "Dogs' faces, together with their ears, tails and soft exterior make them good at expressing emotions. In addition, dogs have a reputation for reliability which makes them ideal for ads wanting to emphasize the very same virtue."

Wow, what a compliment. Where do I sign up? I can sell something. I was in an ad for sterling silver jewelry once. I think I can sell a vacuum cleaner, and I know I can knock over plants.

I have great ears, Mister and Lady always say so. My tail is in excellent shape, having rarely been stepped on and never caught in a closing door. My exterior is very soft, especially after a bath with horse shampoo. Do I sense another canine career on the horizon?

We've had more than one guest make a reservation because they FINALLY put my photo and my own page on the Web site. That's good advertising. An innkeeper dog lying on the porch, sitting attentively during check-in and otherwise contributing to the overall ambiance can enhance a B&B's image immensely. At least to all except perhaps a die-hard cat lover, and then one must consider if a devoted cat lover should be allowed on the premises anyway.

The greatest advertising medium for B&Bs in this day is the Internet. It really levels the playing field for lodging properties, since an inn can have as nice a presentation and be as easy to find as a large hotel.

Guidebooks in our business are probably second to the Internet for advertising. There's always a place for a book. I surely hope so, as I'm spending so much of my nap time on this one! We buy our little blurb in some of these books, many of which are also online. Don't be surprised that we buy the space. We also write the copy. The descriptions are hardly objective, but they are usually pretty accurate.

A few books are not paid ads, like Lady's *Small-Town Restaurants in Virginia*. She actually went to every restaurant and chose which ones to include in the book and which ones were not up to her standards.

Keep an eye out for other small-town restaurant books - she's talking about writing about other states when she finishes editing my work and touring with me. I'm not sure if that's before or after her *Observations of a Trucker Dog* which will explore the over-the-road trucking industry and if those drivers really survive on gravy and biscuits and mashed potatoes.

There's my advertising for future books, neatly stuffed into the Advertising chapter. Told you I could sell something.

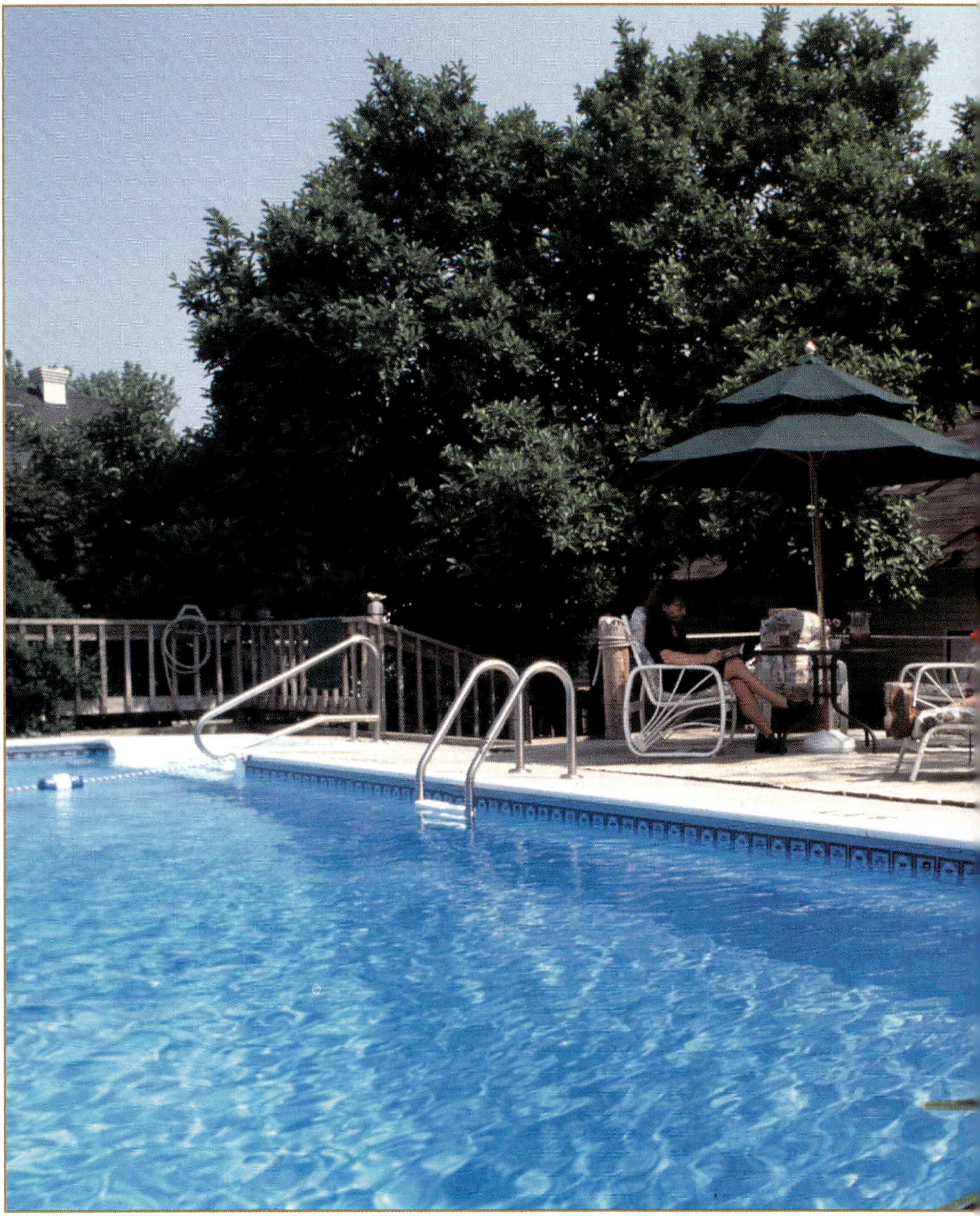

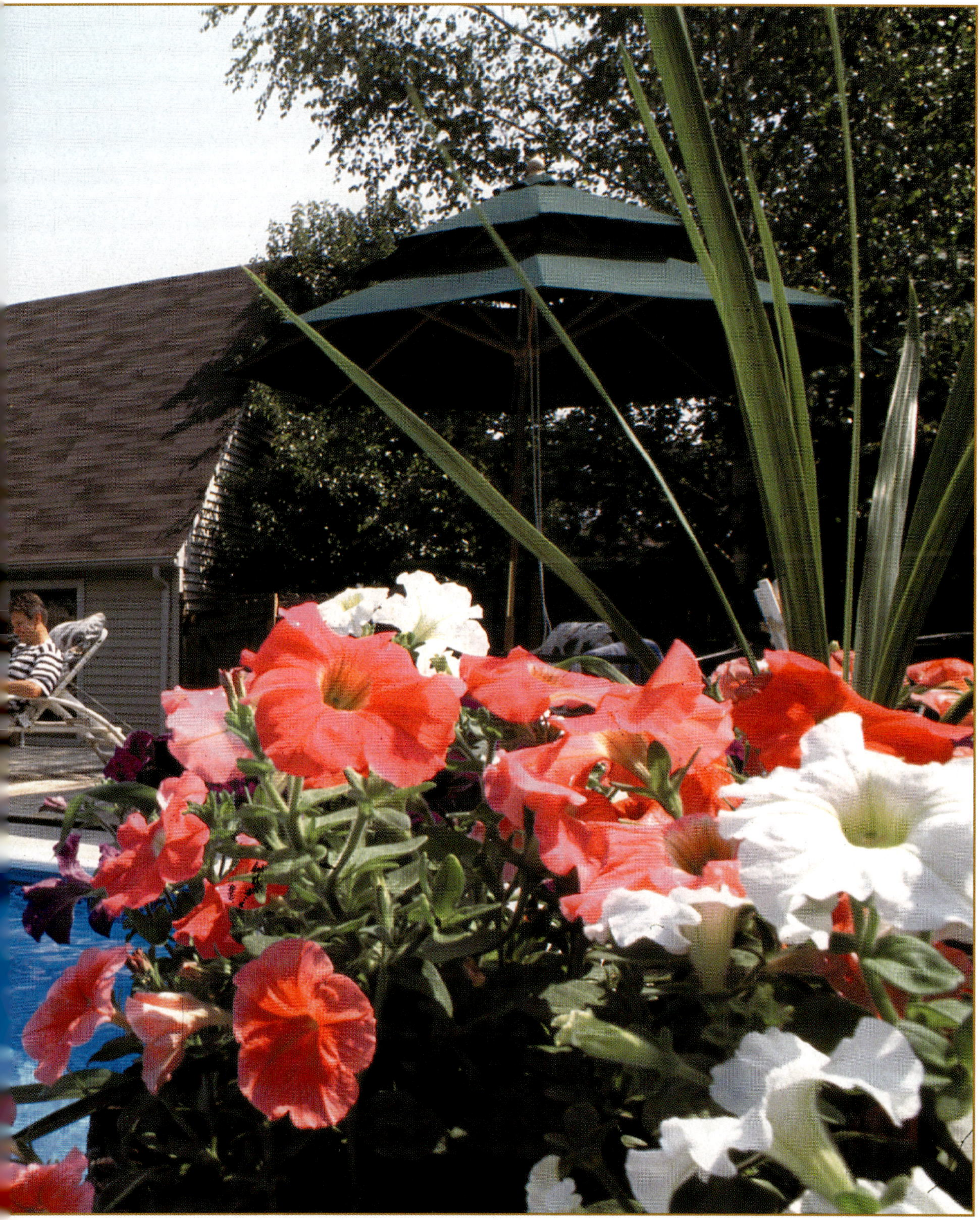

33

Media Relations

I've been in newspapers four times —- two articles, one advertisement and a photo of Mister and me on our morning ride. He rides, I run. I have also been on television.

Lady's writing career was launched with the first article she sold, "60 Minutes is Here – Are You Ready?" about media management during a crisis.

My personal newspaper experience was very short. I got kicked out of the New River Valley Bureau office of *The Roanoke Times* when I was a puppy.

Lady took me to work – part of my Leader Dog training. I did not behave, not for one minute. Not even for one half-minute. After a couple of days of that, then-editor Beth Obenshain put her foot down. Not on me. She laid the law about having – not having, as it were – dogs at the newspaper office during the work day.

Lady loved working at the newspaper. It's the only job she has had where she could arrive at work, make a cup of tea and read the morning paper from cover to cover. One of her big goals after retiring from innkeeping is to read a morning newspaper – in the morning – the same morning as the date on the paper.

Newspapers are useful when toys are scarce or boredom sets in. Tearing up a newspaper section or two provides decent, short-term entertainment. Chasing pages outside on a windy day is fun. Even seeing the look of astonishment on Mister and Lady's faces is amusing.

"When WILL you grow up?" they ask. I am then equally astonished that they continue to fail to grasp the reality that the aging Labrador, speaking generally for all the Labrador population, still has lots of puppy inside.

We had a video spot on Time Out one Saturday on WDBJ Channel 7, the CBS channel in Roanoke. Time Out is a three-minute segment where reporter Jennifer Meile shows and talks about some place to go that's nearby. She chose Clay Corner Inn. I was on that little segment THREE times, and Jennifer even talked about this book!

No one has written a magazine article about Clay Corner Inn. We don't know any travel writers, and Blacksburg is not exactly a tourist destination, so travel writers are not inclined to come here.

In our second year, Lady wrote five press releases, assembled photos and information and put together press kits which she mailed to several magazines. She got no response. That's one reason I'm writing this book. To bring some attention to Clay Corner Inn.

I'm going to send free books to media people and book reviewers so I can be in more newspaper articles and TV shows. For television, I think I'll carry a book to the interviewer, and then relax while Lady does the talking. Our junior innkeeper dog, Kent, will come along, too, I think.

Newspapers, magazines and television and radio shows need to fill their pages and minutes every day with something. Any B&B with news that's interesting – like a new innkeeper dog, perhaps, or an award – should notify local and regional media with information and quality photos.

For travel articles, one must remember that most inns are places to stay, but not destinations. Thus, one needs to incorporate local events, attractions and reasons for a traveler to come to where the inn is located.

As I've said many a time, a good innkeeper dog can tilt the decision to stay at a specific B&B. Maybe some writer or editor will also be favorably impressed because innkeeper dog photos are part of your story package. *C'est possible.*

Dealing with the media is like most business relationships – be honest, respect deadlines, give more information than not enough, use layman's language and avoid answering hypothetical questions.

Dealing with dogs is similar – be honest, respect our needs, give more praise than not enough, use simple words and a gentle tone of voice and avoid asking hypothetical questions. And don't expect Labradors to grow up very fast.

34

Names

You can call a dog anything you want, and it will still love and adore you. Leader Dogs for the Blind suggests that you name a dog something that's not a common human name. I'm named after a special king in the Bible.

God said, "Ask for whatever you want me to give you." (I Kings 3:5 NIV)

Solomon responded, "…a discerning heart to govern your people and to distinguish between right and wrong." (I Kings 3:9 NIV)

God said, "Since you have asked for this and not for long life or wealth for yourself … I will give you a wise and discerning heart." (I Kings 3:11, 12 NIV)

God gave Solomon wisdom and very great insight, and a breadth of understanding as measureless as the sand on the seashore. (I Kings 4:29 NIV)

Mister and Lady thought wisdom would play an important role in my life as a Leader Dog. And indeed it would have, but it hasn't been lost in my current positions as Innkeeper Dog and Writer Dog.

It takes some degree of wisdom and discretion to decide what to write and what to leave out of this book, for example. I could tell you stories of things people tell me; things I hear at the breakfast tables; stupid things I've seen guests do or say; stupid things the innkeepers have done.

Why don't I do this? Wisdom, dear friends. I know from whence my bread is buttered, and I'm not about to jeopardize my jobs.

I did not recognize my name for several weeks. Not because I couldn't hear, but in part because I didn't associate the name with me and partly because I had trouble paying attention. Puppies are very busy little creatures, and we much prefer to take information via our little noses than our little floppy ears. I still have a small problem with attention sometimes.

Clay Corner Inn was called Per Diem Bed & Breakfast when the first owners, Vic and Jo Pat Huggins, opened it in 1991. Jo Pat thought it was cute, and it is. Unfortunately, several other connotations were implied. For one, Perdiem all-one-word is the brand name of a laxative. The per diem travel rate for government and military is among the cheapest in the land.

Upon arrival, one guest said:

Oh, what a N-I-C-E place. I told my wife just before we got here that the only room I could find was at a bed and breakfast called Per Diem. I told her not to expect much more than a bed and a chair because it's probably a cheap place for government travelers.

Another asked: *Are you owned by Virginia Tech or some other government entity?* Lady's response: "You think we work this hard for someone else?" Still another person stated: *Let me see, hmmmm, per diem means by day. Can someone stay more than one day? I need a 2-night reservation.*

Then there was a woman who gushed: *Oh my, don't change the name. I love it. It's so-o-o-o-o-o French!* Actually, it's Latin for *by day*, but Lady didn't say so.

There are a few considerations when naming a bed and breakfast, or any business for that matter. Pronunciation, spelling, how it will fit or look on a sign or logo. It's difficult for everyone when a name is not easily understood and must constantly be spelled for clarification.

While I am not listing some of the odd ones I've come across (using wisdom again), here are some of my favorites: Teddy Bear House, Anchorage, AK; Sled Dog Inn, Flagstaff, AZ (what are sled dogs doing in Arizona?); Black Dog Inn, Estes Park, CO; Teddy Bear B&B, Bridgeville, DE; Bears Inn, Evergreen, CO; Foxes in Sutter Creek, Sutter Creek, CA; 1887 Black Dog Inn, Monticello, IN.

35

Writing

We are all writers - me, Mister, Lady and even Kent who wrote one chapter. Mister holds some patents and has published extremely boring articles on electronics stuff, fiber optics technology and such. Everyone knows that Lady writes, and if you're reading this book, you are appreciating canine talent.

Our favorite quote about writing, especially as it applies to describing a B&B or inn property, is this one from Strunk and White's *Elements of Style*:

When you overstate, the reader will be instantly on guard, and everything that has preceded your overstatement as well as everything that follows it will be suspect in his or her mind. A single overstatement, wherever or however it occurs, diminishes the whole, and a single carefree superlative has the power to destroy, for the reader, the object of the writer's enthusiasm.

There is one BIG exception to this rule about overstating and it can be understated in nine letters: Dave Barry. His overstating is generally amusing, even if no one believes some of what he writes. And by the way, what happened to Ernst, the main dog and what's-his-name, the back-up dog? One reads more in his column about what to name a rock group than about his canine companions, if he still has some, IF – and it's a big IF – they haven't tired of his overstating antics.

Things are much different in the B&B world than in his *Miami Herald* humor world. We can't overstate anything without risking a guest's disappointment. Words like *breathtaking, magnificent* and *spectacular* should be avoided — unless, of course, every guest room faces the highest peaks of the Grand Tetons from less than five miles or there are acres of kittens or puppies with whom to play. The latter would definitely qualify as spectacular.

Breakfast may be scrumptious, and the place may be simply adorable, but it's nice to leave those things for the guest to discover. They'll find out, if it really is. It's advisable to spell accommodations and all other words correctly, as well as to avoid redundant phrases like *originally built* and *king size bed*. Even I know that "king" in *king bed* refers to the size. What else? Who's in it? What innkeeper would rent a room where there's a king in the bed?

Writing isn't difficult, especially if you don't try to write. You must act as if you're carrying on a conversation with a friend, except you're writing what you would say instead of actually barking, uh, talking.

Writing is often simply a discipline problem. Forcing oneself to take or make the time to write is a challenge. Imagine how I've managed to squash this book in between my naps and myriad responsibilities at Clay Corner Inn. If I can do it, so can you.

Innkeepers need to write brochures, Web site information, letters, press releases, policies and procedures for guests and for employees, guide book information, articles, dog books – well, some parts of dog books, maybe, but not whole dog books. No, no. The dog must be a major contributor to his or her own book. *Comme moi.*

36

Photography

The photo sessions for this book were fun. I got more treats than in a month of Sundays. Sit, stay, down, look this way, move over, turn around, jump up, jump down, left two inches, right six inches, pick it up, put it down. Exhausting, but treat-laden, therefore fulfilling – or just filling.

The food shoots were just as time-consuming with our photographer, Andy, moving a fork or turning a plate a fraction of an inch this way and that way. Lady read that photographing food is not as simple as one might think. That's easy to believe with the time Andy spent shooting one waffle. One very patient waffle, I might add, compared to me.

Professional photography is an art and a science coupled with a keen eye for color and contrast, angles, lighting, backgrounds, foregrounds, side grounds, coffee grounds. Oops – where's the editor? Error-alert. Delete side grounds and coffee grounds.

Along with a bundle of talent and skill, professional photographers come with a van load of expensive equipment. Cameras, lenses, umbrellas, poles, cords, lights, film, tripods, padded cases and boxes. My limited experience indicates that they don't want dogs poking their noses into the equipment bags or on their lenses. They don't want their extension cords chewed or re-arranged either.

During Kent's first photo shoot, he repeatedly grabbed the lens-cleaning chamois cloth in one of Andy's photo bags. Good dog, I said, and someone moved the bag - or the dog. I don't remember.

Professional photographs are worth the expense in any business, and especially for B&Bs where one is trying to capture an atmosphere to sell an experience. Your image is connected to your photographs. They can be the deciding factor in favor of – or against - making a reservation. My photo on our Web site gets us lots of reservations.

Lady hired an amateur to photograph her small wedding to Mister, and she got what she paid for - a bunch of bad, blurry, blue-ish, bland photos from a boondoggling blunder that blemished beyond belief an event befitting something better.

Wow, what brought on that barrage of batty banter and baloney beginning with B? On the bright side, Lady still has Mister, and that's more valuable than some old photos of how great they looked in younger years.

Professional photographs of an inn, guest rooms, food and innkeeper dogs can be used in many places – obviously, brochures, Web sites and post cards. Convention and visitor bureaus and various tourism agencies are often seeking quality photos for their color publications.

Newspaper and magazine editors are attracted to great photographs before reading an article. If the photo is wonderful, the copy is worth a look. If the photo does not appeal, the copy might not even be read.

And last, but definitely not least, would you have picked up this book if it weren't filled with delightful, professionally shot photographs of me? Maybe yes, maybe no. Probably not.

Kent

37

Tipping

    Tips come my way in various shapes and forms. Lori Wagner brought me a wonderful, stuffed hot dog, complete with roll and fake mustard. I got all the mustard stuff off in a matter of minutes, but the hot dog lives on in my toy basket as an all-time favorite.

    Norris and Nita Monk of Newport News use football games as their excuse to come see me. They gave me an orange Virginia Tech bandanna to wear for special events like football game days and graduation. It looks good, and I'm not allowed to chew on it.

    One guest actually mailed me a multi-color tennis ball. It was as wonderful a gift as the box it came in. I chewed them both. I get steak scraps sometimes and someone once brought me a muffin, a store-bought muffin. Mister and Lady wouldn't let me have the muffin, though. I think because it was store-bought and not homemade. Well, they don't like me eating homemade muffins either, come to think of it. Frankly, I have enough stuff. I really like attention most of all.

    The innkeepers don't get tips either. Occasionally, if they make special arrangements and go above-and-beyond what is expected, someone will give them a tip, but it's never expected. In the same way, one doesn't normally tip the owner of restaurant.

    Since breakfast is part of the B&B rate and part of the deal, tips are not really appropriate at breakfast either. Housekeepers at B&Bs and inns are often better paid than those who work in hotels and motels, but they are the service staff, and tips are always welcome for their hard work.

    Cleaning rooms is not very glamorous work, and the world over, housekeep-

Photo by author

ers are the least recognized and some of the most valuable staff at lodging establishments. Consider this:

If a front desk clerk is a little snippy at check-in, you'll probably overlook it. If the bellman drops one of your bags on the way to your room, you'll probably overlook that. If a waitress brings you coffee instead of tea, you'll probably make the correction. If the innkeeper dog doesn't get up to greet you in full wag and wiggle, you might even be OK.

Any number of little gaffes can be accepted, BUT if your room is dirty, you will NOT be happy and you may never come back. *C'est vrai.*

38

Health & Well-Being

It's very important in our positions that we be healthy, well-rested and in good shape to carry out our responsibilities. I like 10 or more hours of sleep every night, so I begin seriously napping right after dinner. I complement that with several naps each day.

Mister and Lady try to retire about 10:30 each night and arise one hour before breakfast begins. They don't actually sleep all this time, however. Sometimes the telephone rings late or someone is locked out of the guest room or a car crashes into a guest house.

Other disruptions include noise from traffic, guest doors opening and closing, differences in temperature control – too hot for Mister, too cold for Lady – or the reverse if there's a hot flash, or flashes, involved.

Just to enlighten you who may not already know this: It's impossible to remain detached from the menopausal experience if it's occurring in the place where you live. I'm happy to report that we got through it successfully. And we're thankful it occurs just once in a lifetime, even though it can drag on for months and deliver unexpected and unexplained bursts of intense emotion, among other things.

We all need exercise, and I take Mister out twice a day. This is not your standard "walk the dog" program. We run. Well, one of us runs. The other usually rides a bicycle or walks.

It begins with the sound of crumpling plastic. That's Mister getting a poopie bag or two. He never leaves home without one. I tear down the three deck steps at about 50 mph, then sit in the driveway and wait. And wait. And wait. Patiently.

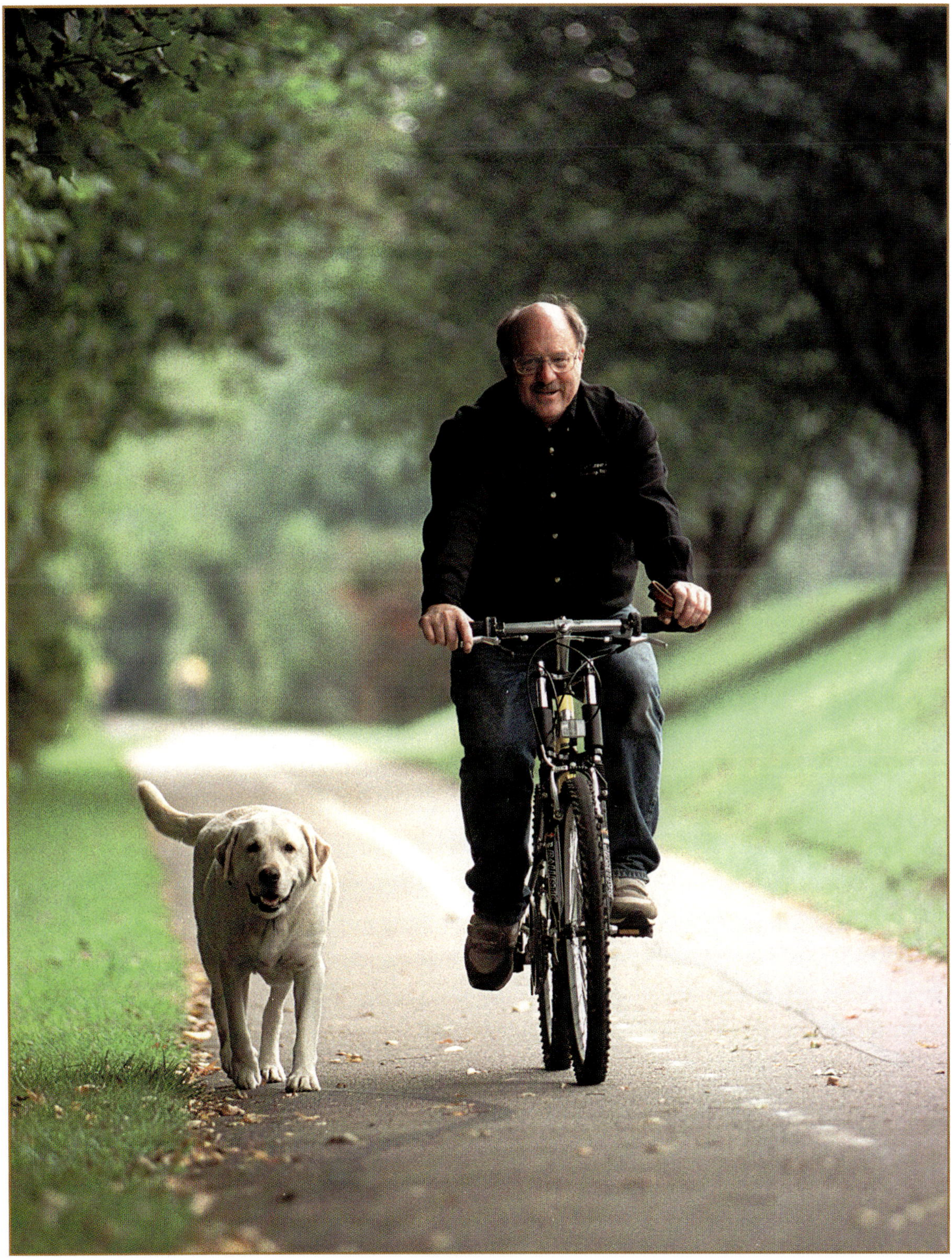

In the early years, Mister kept me on a leash while he rode the bike. I was trained to heel to a person or grocery cart, so I heeled to the bicycle. Well, sort of. Until I spotted an irresistible chase. Then I would take off at breakneck speed, which wreaked havoc for man and bicycle. They became instantly separated, and I was tethered to it all, so that didn't work well for anyone. Except, of course, the object of the chase.

This regular exercise, along with a little training, contributes to my calm demeanor around the inn. Dogs need lots of exercise, especially us Labradors. We are working dogs and need physical and mental stimulation.

Being a full-time pet is OK, but we still need to run, jump, play, sniff and have

Photo by author

activities that challenge us. Innkeeper dog is an excellent position, and I think I would have made a good Leader Dog. I like to be busy and productive.

I have bilateral hip dysplasia – that's why I'm not in a dog guide job. I take an aspirin dissolved in water each morning, along with a couple glucosamine sulphate vitamins tossed in my food. The aspirin thing is Mister's idea. He thinks the reason people have stomach trouble with aspirin is because they swallow the whole piece.

"Aspirin is merely a clump of acid," I've heard him say, "and naturally it's going to eat a hole in your stomach." So we all drink our aspirin in my pack.

We drink lots of water, eat well-balanced diets, try to maintain good weights

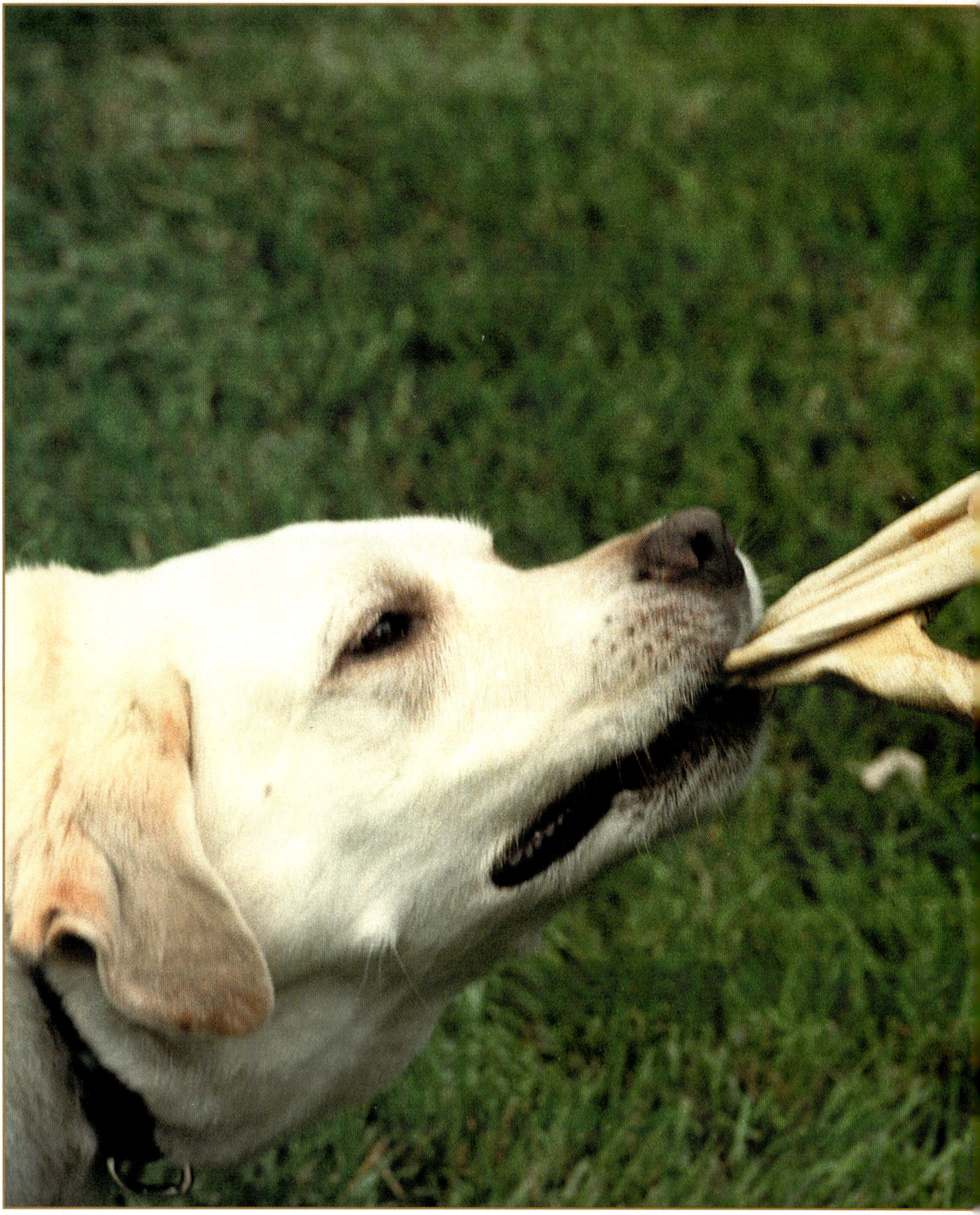

and get regular check-ups. Mister and Lady eat too much candy and chocolate. I get too few treats. Mister cleans my ears and teeth (and his own) often. I love to be brushed, and my fur can be buffed nicely with a chamois cloth.

I perform some grooming on my own by licking. Typical of most retrievers, I can get stuck licking and just keep lapping my paw or the rug or floor. It's usually Lady who stops me with "don't-lapyourpaws." That's not a typo – it sounds like one word to me, and I've heard it more than 10,000 times, I think.

Some dogs take anti-anxiety drugs to control "lick granuloma" – the technical term for lapping too much. Others take drugs for separation anxiety and a host of other things. Lady knows about anxiety. She's had agoraphobia since she was 13. But she doesn't take any drugs, and she won't allow me to either. We are *personnes – ou les chiens – au naturel.*

Innkeepers are high energy people who think they can do it all. And they can do a lot. But they need rest and relaxation sometimes, too. Some of the signs I have observed that signal overworked innkeepers include indulging in copious amounts of the little chocolates purchased for guests, being short-tempered with the innkeeper dog, walking past the innkeeper dog in a huff, forgetting to brush the innkeeper dog, not petting and entertaining the innkeeper dog for long periods of time – those kinds of things. Studies show that petting a dog can lower blood pressure, so that's real good for all of us.

39

Innsitting

Innsitting is a real job performed by real people. I think there's even a professional innsitters association. It's a good way to learn the business before risking one's life savings on a property.

The term appears to be a variation of babysitting, a logical concept since one really can just sit with a baby, a sleeping one anyway. Before we bought the B&B, we had a housesitter who doubled as a dogsitter.

Now we have innsitters, and I'm here to tell you, there's no sitting going on at this inn. Alan and Marilyn Elliott can heartily attest to that. This wonderful couple came from Harrisonburg several times over a couple years to innsit and dogsit for up to two weeks.

Here's how things unfolded for them. Lady would call them a few months in advance. "It'll be easy," she'd say. "Looks like we have only a couple guests during that week."

By the time they arrived, however, we were usually in a sell-out situation, more than a couple dozen guests, some who may or may not speak much English, extra breakfasts scheduled on several mornings — everything running at full tilt and one unpredictable staffing problem.

"Welcome, Alan and Marilyn, we're so glad you're here," Lady would say through a tired smile. "We're a little busier than I thought we would be."

I could see their unspoken response, "So what else is new?" This happened almost every time they came. They took it all in stride and managed to keep the place together and operating quite well.

Our regular guests enjoyed seeing them and learning that Mister and Lady did take a break once in a while, even if without me. I carried on with my regular duties, in addition to getting into as much mischief as I could find. I walked Alan twice a day, when I picked up my dish he fed me, we played ball, and he met some of my friends. You see, my job never ends. If it's not backing up Lady and Mister, it's training the innsitters.

Innsitters come from all walks of life. Many of them are former innkeepers who want to keep their hands in the business without owning one; others are aspiring innkeepers who innsit for experience. Still others, like Alan and Marilyn, are just nice, personable folks who earn extra money and enjoy the hospitality experience.

Of course, I chip in where I can with extra maintenance and clean up help during these times.

Innsitter people are very important to innkeepers, especially for inns like ours that rarely close. In fact, keeping the inn open and generating revenue is the main reason for hiring innsitters.

Another reason for having innsitters, flimsy as it is, is that they are possibly the only people in the world who can fully appreciate an innkeeper's job. And it's nice to be appreciated.

40

Vacation

In the summer of 1999, after I received the 16th (of 22) rejection for publishing this book, Mister decided that Lady needed a complete vacation of rest - no working. But he thought I should work on the book during this time, so he made arrangements with B&Bs and a country inn that do not generally accept pets to allow me to stay. And he further stated that I would write a chapter about this adventure, so here's my first (and possibly last) "What I Did on My Summer Vacation."

First overnight stop was Village Farm Bed & Breakfast in Carlisle, PA. I made quick note of the brick farmhouse, outbuildings and fields before locking eyes with a big orange cat on the porch. A little terrier type dog came out the front door, followed by a medium-sized retriever mix. I liked the place immediately.

The dogs were very friendly and happy to see me. We sniffed, peed, sniffed and peed for a while. The women chatted and Mister took me and Tessa, the mix, to the cornfield where I scared up a rabbit.

When I got into the house, I saw many things at my level, so I gently picked up one doll. It was obvious by Lady's reaction that these were not dog toys, so I released it and refrained from re-arranging the others. It was a warm night, so rather than sleep on my sheet on top of a soft Oriental rug, I spent a cool night on the bathroom tile floor.

Breakfast was served outside, and I was leashed at the table and forced to lie down less than three feet from a water garden. This is akin to placing an unwrapped piece of chocolate in front of Mister or Lady and saying "don't touch it, you can't have it" and then making them sit there for one hour.

Colleen Scott, 9

Photo by Author

The air was fresh, the food apparently delicious (I wouldn't know), the conversation went on for more than an hour, and generally speaking, a good time was had by all.

The next five nights we stayed at the Dorset Inn in Dorset, Vermont -one of Lady's favorite towns in her home state. There are four dogs here - Fergie the basset, Chloe and Whitman the chocolate Labradors, and Reba the black Labrador - all cordial, except Whitman, the oldest, but not overbearing and decidedly not interested in playing with me. I watched them the first morning sit with chef/owner Sissy Hicks for a photograph for the cover of her cookbook, *Flavors from the Heart.* Good dogs they were, if a little on the dull side.

But there was nothing dull about our first morning outing. Mister and I walked down the highway a bit and turned up a country lane. We were walking on a slight incline up the road when we noticed a tall animal sauntering down the road. Mister isn't afraid of anything so I scooted over closer to him. But I felt his body tense a little. We stopped and this 7-foot high, 4-footed fluffy friendly-looking creature just kept coming.

At about two feet, it stopped. We stopped. There we stood in the middle of a Vermont back road looking at each other, wondering what to do next. Then a man appeared with a cup of food, trying to entice his llama back into the fenced area behind a barn on our left. A llama!! A curious, gentle, unusual, slobbering llama! A llama, we were informed, who likes dogs, even after being bitten by a German Shepherd.

There was an older yellow Lab named Tinkerbell on the little town green across from the inn every day. We exchanged sniffs and dog pleasantries once or twice. Otherwise, we walked and read and shopped.

I'm partial to the Orvis store because I'm allowed inside, and the dog department is right inside the front door. I sniffed everything, but didn't pick up anything. I was so sure they'd buy me something. But they didn't. Not this time. I have Orvis stuff already.

A wee-bit-of-thing dog came in as we were leaving. Lady murmured something about "lunch meat," and Mister was just about to comment that it looked more like a cat when I noticed the look on the little doggie's owner's face. I dragged them both out of the store before more damage occurred to the little doggie's ego or the woman's self-esteem.

After five days of doing almost nothing, we went to cousin Mary's house in Waterbury, Vermont, for a night. I was kept separated from a cat, so this short visit was uneventful. The black Labrador next door dropped in for a treat. Mary keeps a jar of dog treats on her porch for him. My kind of neighbor, Mary is.

The next day we attended a family reunion in northern Vermont. I spent all my time with the children. They were lots of fun, but the adults, many admitted cat lovers among them, just stood or sat around drinking various concoctions, talking, talking, talking and looking at old photographs. The kids were neat, and we spent that night in a hotel in Rutland, about an hour down the road.

Lunch the next day was at Lady's great-Aunt Sally's in Cambridge, NY. Lady's brother met us there, and it was the first time in more than 30 years that this brother and sister who jumped in hay mows, shucked corn, learned to tie their shoes and sang to sheep as children were together again with their beloved Aunt Sally. She was very gracious to me, and I can see why being in her presence is very special. She's my Aunt Sally now, too, I think, sort of.

We drove to Carlisle, PA, that afternoon and spent the night at Pheasant Farm B&B, one of the most beautiful B&Bs any of us have visited. I wasn't allowed in the main house, but it was really pretty from the outside, and Mister and Lady raved about the inside. There were horses in the fields, a great horse barn next to our cottage and gorgeous grounds. I couldn't go in the horse barn or pasture, but I did walk around outside and refrain from chasing their cat.

It was restful for Lady, as Mister wanted it. I was the only one working.

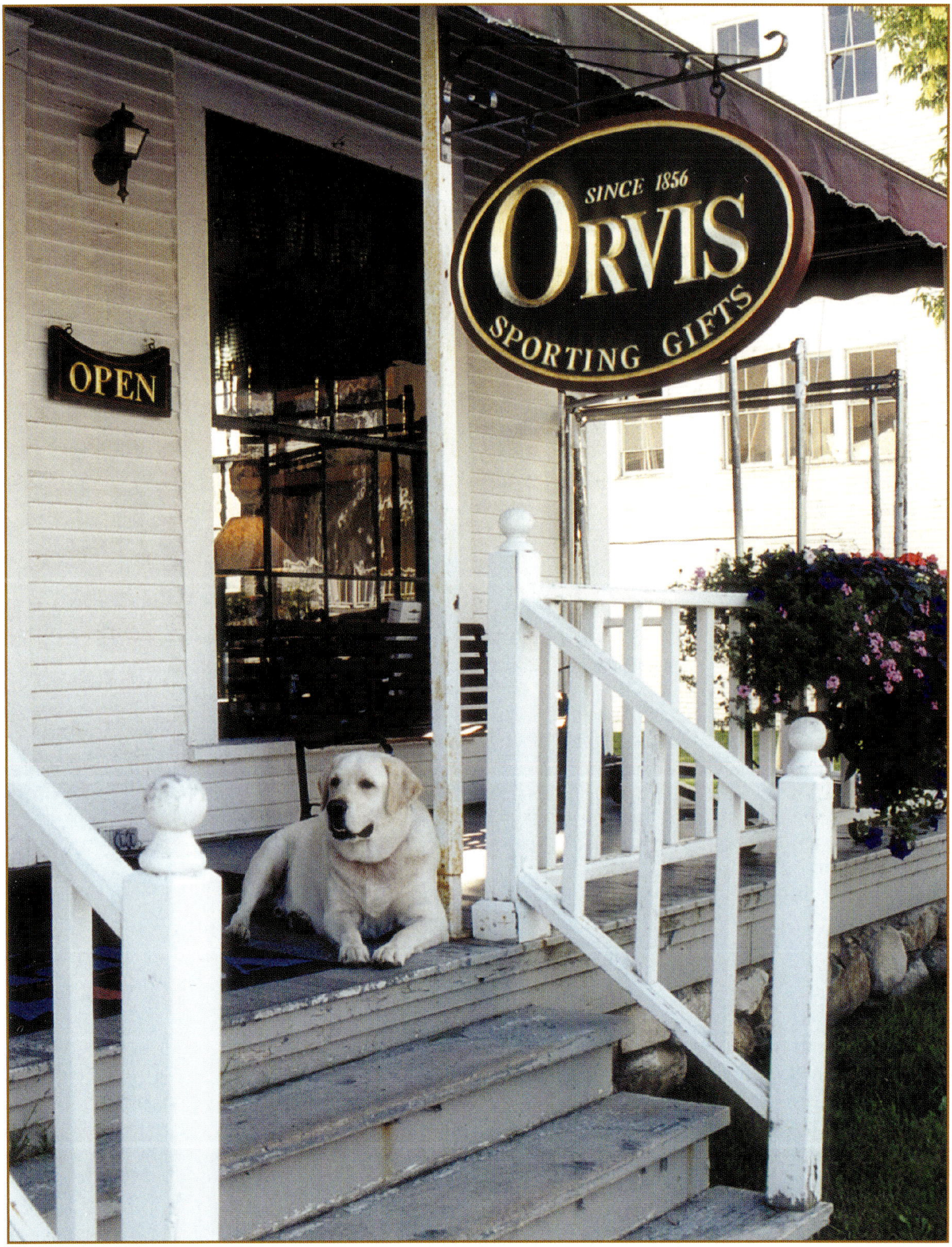
OPEN
SINCE 1856
ORVIS
SPORTING GIFTS

41

The Future of Innkeeping

Innkeeping is one of the oldest lines of work, and it's likely that people will always travel and need lodging. The B&B industry has evolved into an appealing lodging option among business and leisure travelers, and it just may have had an impact on its larger counterparts.

Have you ever wondered why hotels started offering free breakfasts? Me neither, really, but others have speculated that one reason people patronize B&Bs is the breakfast part. I am certainly persuaded to go where there's food over some place *sans repas*.

My simple outlook on the future is the three I's: Innkeeper dogs, Internet, and Increased professionalism.

Innkeeper dogs should become more important and more visible, and hopefully, much more appreciated with the advent of my personal publicity campaign explaining the myriad responsibilities and chores laid upon at least one innkeeper dog – *moi*.

I accept my position joyfully, along with the added job of training Kent, and look forward to a future of continued hospitality service.

The Internet may have been a boon to B&Bs more than any other class of lodging properties. Advertising is too expensive for small inns, and word of mouth is limited since a small percentage of the traveling public stay at bed and breakfast inns. The World Wide Web provides exposure for everyone regardless of size, and lots more people are using the Internet to explore lodging options.

Along with increased professionalism come more rooms per property, wired rooms, "green" policies, more amenities and better flexibility. To make a living,

I've heard one needs at least eight rooms or more, depending on location, occupancy and rates. Many people becoming innkeepers now have business experience and opportunities to innsit and attend seminars and classes.

Because innkeepers are more professional, they understand the attraction of cable TV, private telephones, data ports, a Web site and e-mail. A firm handshake and professional attitude, coupled with an innkeeper dog or two and some common sense, will put anyone on the right track.

We recycle whatever we can, even the soda bottles I've chewed on. I'm partial to the 20-ounce plastic ones; they make quite a crunch while squashing them with my teeth. I can also throw and chase them. I took one off a table once with soda still in it. I trotted around the room with it so the soda didn't all fall in one place. After the fact – and Lady's reaction - I don't think this was the best approach to emptying the bottle.

We started a policy of not changing towels every day if they're hanging up and changing them if they're on the floor. I personally like to use the same towel for about a month, and I even share it. Not so with people.

Flexibility applies to everything from check-in and check-out times to breakfast hours and cancellation policies. I'm a laid-back, easy-going, don't-get-ruffled-about-little-things kind of dog, and I try to run the place so it reflects my personality. I'm also very clean and neat-appearing, and those qualities overflow into all of our guest rooms and common spaces.

Lots of people, like guests Charles and Karen Blankenship of Powhatan, Virginia, have turned to bed and breakfast inns as warmer, more friendly and more interesting places to stay. "I don't know what I'd do if I had to stay in a hotel again," Karen said on their last visit.

Her comments have been echoed by many of our guests, and that bodes well for the future of innkeeping.

EPILOGUE

Two major events occurred shortly before this book went to press. We moved into a little house at the back of the property - our own two-bedroom cottage. It's very nice to have a place where we can really relax, even sleep late sometimes. And with Kent, there are four in my pack now – too many for one small room.

I had knee surgery on my right leg, as you can see in this photo (taken in our new living room). My fur will grow back by book tour time. I'm told that I'll be able to walk on this leg comfortably again. And I will be able to play with Kent and chase rabbits after eight long, slow, hard, boring weeks just walking on a leash.

Solomon

Kent

Joanne M. Anderson's articles have appeared in national and regional magazines, and her book, *Small-Town Restaurants in Virginia*, John F. Blair Publisher, is in its second printing.

She graduated from the University of Georgia and holds a diploma from the Educational Institute of the American Hotel and Lodging Association with specialization in food and beverage management.

A Vermont native, Anderson was attracted to the innkeeping lifestyle for many years. In the mid-1980s, she changed careers from high tech to hospitality. A decade later, she and her husband, John, bought the bed and breakfast that has become Clay Corner Inn.

"The Newhart Show also influenced me to become an innkeeper and writer," she quips. "And fortunately, I do not have Larry and Darryl and Darryl for neighbors."

Born in Havana, Cuba in 1952, Andres R. Alonso moved to Fairfax, VA, when his family was forced to leave Cuba in 1961. While his work takes him all over the country, he currently resides with his wife and two children in Roanoke, VA.

He became a professional photographer in 1982 working for *The Northern Virginia Sun and The Loudoun Times-Mirror*. In 1986 he became a freelance, contract photographer for *The Washington Post*. Since then, his work has appeared in many national publications including *The New York Times, USA Today, Newsweek, Time, and The Los Angeles Times.* His clients include *Marriott, Norfolk Southern, American Express* and *First Union National Bank*.

His photographs have been used by the *Associated Press, Agence-France Presse, CBS Television*, the *NCAA* and many colleges and universities in the mid-Atlantic region, and they were featured in NASCAR's 50th anniversary book *Thunder in America*. He has self-published one book, *Martinsville Speedway: Half-Mile of Thunder*.

125

Solomon Says: Observations of an Innkeeper Dog
Quick Order Form

Telephone orders: (540) 951-0809, have your credit card ready.
Fax orders: (540) 951-0541, use this form.
Postal orders: Clay Corner Publishing, 401 Clay Street SW, Blacksburg, VA 24060, use this form.

Please send _____ books @ $24.95 each.
Name _____
Street address _____
City, State, ZIP _____
Telephone (_____) _____

Books ordered with this form will be pawtographed and autographed and signed TO someone special if printed clearly below. If you do not want books unwrapped and signed, circle this: DO NOT SIGN BOOKS

Print clearly.
Sign book TO: _____
Sign book TO: _____
Sign book TO: _____

Sales tax: Add 4.5% for books shipped to Virginia addresses.
Shipping/handling: $4 for first book and $2 for each additional book

Payment: _____ check enclosed
_____ VISA _____ MasterCard _____ American Express
Credit card # _____ Exp date _____
Name on card _____ (please print)
Signature _____

Solomon Says: Observations of an Innkeeper Dog
Quick Order Form

Telephone orders: (540) 951-0809, have your credit card ready.
Fax orders: (540) 951-0541, use this form.
Postal orders: Clay Corner Publishing, 401 Clay Street SW, Blacksburg, VA 24060, use this form.

Please send _____ books @ $24.95 each.
Name _____
Street address _____
City, State, ZIP _____
Telephone (_____) _____

Books ordered with this form will be pawtographed and autographed and signed TO someone special if printed clearly below. If you do not want books unwrapped and signed, circle this: DO NOT SIGN BOOKS

Print clearly.
Sign book TO: _____
Sign book TO: _____
Sign book TO: _____

Sales tax: Add 4.5% for books shipped to Virginia addresses.
Shipping/handling: $4 for first book and $2 for each additional book

Payment: _____ check enclosed
_____ VISA _____ MasterCard _____ American Express
Credit card # _____ Exp date _____
Name on card _____ (please print)
Signature _____